Digital Literacy in the Fourth Industrial Revolution: Navigating the Future with Essential Skills

By

Natasha Able

About the Author

Natasha Able is a versatile writer with a boundless curiosity for the world. Her interests span across culture, sports, technology, music, entertainment, politics, economics, and international relations. With a strong background as a researcher at a leading think tank specializing in tech policy and societal changes, Natasha brings a unique perspective to her writing on global trends and developments.

Natasha's deep understanding of technology stems from her work at the forefront of tech policy discussions, where she explores the implications of emerging technologies on society and governance. Her insights into the intersection of technology and public policy provide readers with comprehensive analyses of complex issues shaping the digital landscape.

In her free time, Natasha indulges her passion for exploration through travel and documentary watching, enriching her understanding of diverse cultures and global issues. An avid photographer, she captures the essence of her journeys, blending her love for visual storytelling with her intellectual pursuits.

Natasha's commitment to exploring and explaining significant developments in technology and beyond ensures that her readers receive engaging, well-informed content that reflects her dedication to understanding the world's most pressing issues.

TABLE OF CONTENTS

Chapter 1:

Introduction to Digital Literacy in the 4th Industrial Revolution

Definition and Importance of Digital Literacy in the Context of the Fourth Industrial Revolution (4IR)

In the digital age, literacy extends far beyond the ability to read and write. Today, digital literacy encompasses a set of competencies required to effectively navigate, understand, and contribute to the digital world. As we usher in the Fourth Industrial Revolution (4IR), characterized by the fusion of physical, digital, and biological spheres, digital literacy has become an essential skill set.

Digital literacy involves more than just using technology; it includes understanding how technology works, critically assessing digital content, communicating effectively using digital platforms, and creating digital content responsibly. It is about empowering individuals to participate fully in the digital society, fostering a sense of digital citizenship.

The 4IR is marked by rapid advancements in artificial intelligence (AI), robotics, the Internet of Things (IoT), quantum computing, and other groundbreaking technologies. These innovations are transforming industries, economies, and our everyday lives. In this context, digital literacy is vital. It enables individuals to adapt to new technologies, enhances employability, and fosters innovation and creativity. It is the key to unlocking the potential of the 4IR for all.

Overview of Global Digital Literacy Levels and the Impact on Economies, Societies, and Individual Empowerment

Globally, digital literacy levels vary significantly. In some regions, digital literacy is widespread, while in others, a digital divide persists, exacerbated by factors such as socioeconomic status, education, age, and geographic location. Understanding these disparities is crucial for developing strategies to enhance digital literacy worldwide.

Impact on Economies

Digital literacy is a driver of economic growth. Economies with high levels of digital literacy tend to be more innovative and competitive. Digital skills are essential in the modern workforce, enabling employees to perform complex tasks, improve productivity, and adapt to technological changes. Companies that leverage digital tools and platforms can streamline operations, reach global markets, and foster innovation. Furthermore, digital literacy supports entrepreneurship by providing individuals with the skills needed to start and grow digital businesses, contributing to economic dynamism.

Impact on Societies

On a societal level, digital literacy promotes social inclusion and equity. It provides access to information, education, healthcare, and other essential services, bridging gaps that often exist in traditional infrastructures. Digital literacy empowers individuals to engage in civic activities, from participating in online discussions to voting in digital elections, thereby strengthening democratic processes. Additionally, it fosters a sense of community and global interconnectedness, allowing people to share ideas, cultures, and experiences across borders.

Individual Empowerment

For individuals, digital literacy is a gateway to personal and professional development. It opens up opportunities for lifelong learning, enabling people to acquire new skills and knowledge continuously. Digital literacy enhances employability, as most modern jobs require some level of digital competence. It also empowers individuals to manage their digital footprint, protecting their privacy and security online. In essence, digital literacy equips individuals with the tools to navigate the complexities of the digital world confidently and responsibly.

Outline of the Book's Structure

This book is designed to provide a comprehensive exploration of digital literacy in the 4IR era. It is structured to guide readers from foundational concepts to advanced applications, ensuring a logical and coherent progression of ideas. Here is an overview of the chapters:

Chapter 1: Introduction to Digital Literacy in the 4th Industrial Revolution

- Definition and importance of digital literacy in the context of the 4IR.
- Overview of global digital literacy levels and the impact on economies, societies, and individual empowerment.
- Outline of the book's structure.

Chapter 2: Global Internet Usage Statistics

- Recent statistics on global internet penetration, mobile phone usage, and digital literacy levels.
- Analysis of significant global trends and disparities in internet access and digital literacy.
- Regional comparisons and highlights of countries with notable advancements or challenges.

Chapter 3: Government Policies on Digital Literacy and Internet Usage

- Overview of various government initiatives, regulations, and policies related to digital literacy, internet access, and cybersecurity worldwide.
- Case studies of successful national digital literacy programs.
- Evaluation of the impact of these policies on digital literacy and societal development.

Chapter 4: Digital Literacy in Education

- How schools and universities globally are integrating digital tools and internet resources into their curricula.
- Success stories and challenges in enhancing education through digital means.
- Role of digital literacy in remote learning, particularly highlighted by the COVID-19 pandemic.

Chapter 5: Remote Work and the Digital Economy

- Exploration of the adoption of remote work globally, accelerated by the COVID-19 pandemic.
- The role of digital literacy in enabling remote work and its impact on the global job market.
- Discussion on digital nomadism and the future of work.

Chapter 6: The Role of Social Media

- Analysis of the global popularity and impact of social media platforms.
- How social media is used for communication, information dissemination, civic engagement, and activism.
- The influence of social media on public opinion, culture, and politics.

Chapter 7: E-Commerce and Digital Literacy

- Growth of e-commerce worldwide and its impact on traditional retail.
- Digital skills required for participating in e-commerce, both as consumers and entrepreneurs.
- Challenges and opportunities for enhancing digital literacy in the context of online shopping and digital marketplaces.

Chapter 8: Digital Assets and Cybersecurity

- Explanation of digital assets (cryptocurrencies, NFTs, etc.) and their relevance to individuals and businesses globally.

- Overview of digital asset management and security practices.
- The role of digital literacy in protecting against cyber threats and ensuring safe online transactions.

Chapter 9: Safe Internet Usage: Addressing Risks

- Risks of internet addiction, its consequences on mental health, and strategies to mitigate these risks.
- Examination of online safety issues such as cyberbullying, privacy concerns, and data breaches.
- Initiatives aimed at promoting safe and responsible internet usage.

Chapter 10: Combating Misinformation and Fake News

- Global spread of misinformation and fake news.
- Impact of misinformation on societies, democracies, and public health.
- Strategies and tools to combat misinformation, including fact-checking initiatives and digital literacy programs.

Chapter 11: Digital Literacy and Inclusivity

- Digital literacy disparities among different demographics, including gender, age, and socioeconomic status.
- Initiatives and programs aimed at bridging the digital divide and promoting digital inclusivity.
- Success stories of marginalized communities gaining empowerment through digital literacy.

Chapter 12: Global Case Studies in Digital Literacy

- Detailed case studies of countries and regions that have made significant strides in digital literacy.
- Lessons learned from successful digital literacy programs and policies.
- Comparative analysis of different approaches to improving digital literacy.

Chapter 13: The Role of Artificial Intelligence in Digital Literacy

- Examination of how AI technologies are being used to enhance digital literacy.
- Case studies of AI-driven educational tools and platforms.
- Ethical implications of using AI in digital education.

Chapter 14: Digital Literacy in Healthcare

- Impact of digital literacy on healthcare access and quality.
- How digital tools are transforming patient care, medical research, and public health.
- Challenges and opportunities in educating the public about digital health resources.

Chapter 15: The Future of Digital Literacy in the 4IR

- Predictions and scenarios for the future development of digital literacy.
- Potential advancements in technology and their implications for digital literacy.
- Philosophical and ethical considerations about the future of human interaction with digital technologies.

Chapter 16: Digital Literacy in Developing Countries

- Challenges and opportunities specific to developing countries in enhancing digital literacy.
- Successful initiatives and programs in developing regions.
- Impact of digital literacy on economic development and poverty reduction.

Chapter 17: Ethical and Legal Considerations in Digital Literacy

- Overview of ethical issues related to digital literacy, including privacy, surveillance, and digital rights.
- Legal frameworks governing digital literacy, internet access, and cybersecurity.
- Role of digital literacy in fostering a responsible and ethical digital society.

By the end of this book, you will gain a comprehensive understanding of digital literacy's critical role in the 4IR, equipped with insights, strategies, and practical knowledge to navigate and contribute to the digital world.

Chapter 2:

Global Internet Usage Statistics

In today's interconnected world, the internet serves as a crucial lifeline for information, communication, and commerce. Understanding the current landscape of global internet usage, mobile phone penetration, and digital literacy levels provides valuable insights into how different regions are adapting to the digital age. This chapter presents the most recent statistics on these topics, analyzes significant trends and disparities, and highlights notable advancements and challenges across various countries.

Recent Statistics on Global Internet Penetration, Mobile Phone Usage, and Digital Literacy Levels

Global Internet Penetration

As of 2023, approximately 5.16 billion people, or 64.4% of the global population, have access to the internet. This figure represents significant growth from previous years, with a notable increase in internet adoption across developing regions. The statistics below provide a breakdown of internet penetration by continent:

- **Asia**: 2.7 billion internet users, representing 64.1% of the population.
- **Africa**: 743 million internet users, representing 53.6% of the population.
- **Europe**: 738 million internet users, representing 89.6% of the population.

- **Latin America and the Caribbean**: 514 million internet users, representing 78.9% of the population.
- **North America**: 349 million internet users, representing 94.6% of the population.
- **Oceania**: 34 million internet users, representing 69.6% of the population.

(Source: International Telecommunication Union, ITU, 2023)

Mobile Phone Usage

Mobile phone usage continues to rise globally, with an estimated 7.33 billion mobile phone users in 2023. Mobile devices have become the primary means of internet access for many, especially in regions with limited broadband infrastructure. Here is the mobile phone penetration by continent:

- **Asia**: 3.5 billion users
- **Africa**: 1.1 billion users
- **Europe**: 750 million users
- **Latin America and the Caribbean**: 450 million users
- **North America**: 350 million users
- **Oceania**: 40 million users

(Source: GSMA Intelligence, 2023)

Digital Literacy Levels

Digital literacy levels vary widely across the globe, influenced by factors such as education systems, economic development, and government policies. Here are some key statistics on digital literacy:

- **Europe**: High digital literacy rates, with over 85% of the population possessing basic digital skills.
- **North America**: Similarly high rates, with about 87% of the population digitally literate.
- **Asia**: Varies significantly; countries like South Korea and Japan have over 80% digital literacy, while others lag behind.
- **Latin America**: Moderate levels, with an average of 55-65% digital literacy.
- **Africa**: Generally lower, with notable disparities; countries like South Africa and Kenya have around 40-50% digital literacy, while others are below 30%.
- **Oceania**: High in countries like Australia and New Zealand, with over 80% digital literacy.

(Source: UNESCO Institute for Statistics, 2023)

Analysis of Significant Global Trends and Disparities in Internet Access and Digital Literacy

Trends in Internet Access

One significant trend is the rapid growth of internet access in developing regions, particularly in Asia and Africa. Mobile internet is driving this growth, with smartphones becoming increasingly affordable and accessible. However, this rapid expansion also highlights disparities:

- **Urban vs. Rural**: Urban areas generally have higher internet penetration and better infrastructure compared to rural areas.
- **Economic Disparities**: Wealthier regions and countries tend to have higher internet penetration and

digital literacy levels. Economic disparities within countries also affect access and literacy.
- **Gender Gap**: In many regions, men have higher internet access and digital literacy rates than women, although efforts are underway to bridge this gap.

Disparities in Digital Literacy

Digital literacy disparities are influenced by education, infrastructure, and socioeconomic factors. Key observations include:

- **Educational Systems**: Countries with strong educational systems often have higher digital literacy rates. Investment in digital education is crucial for improving literacy levels.
- **Infrastructure**: Reliable internet infrastructure is essential for digital literacy. Regions with poor infrastructure struggle with both access and literacy.
- **Government Policies**: Effective government policies and initiatives can significantly improve digital literacy. Countries with strong digital literacy programs tend to have better outcomes.

Regional Comparisons and Highlights of Countries with Notable Advancements or Challenges

Africa

- **Kenya**: Kenya has made significant strides in digital literacy through initiatives like the Digital Literacy Programme, which aims to integrate ICT into primary education. Mobile money platforms like M-Pesa have also driven digital literacy and financial inclusion.

- **South Africa**: With relatively high internet penetration, South Africa has focused on enhancing digital skills through programs like the National Digital Skills Framework. However, disparities between urban and rural areas remain a challenge.
- **Nigeria**: Nigeria faces challenges with infrastructure but has a burgeoning tech scene in cities like Lagos. Initiatives like the National Digital Economy Policy are aimed at improving digital literacy.
- **Uganda**: Uganda has seen growth in mobile internet usage. Programs like the National ICT Initiatives Support Programme (NIISP) aim to enhance digital skills, though rural areas still lag behind.

Asia

- **South Korea**: South Korea boasts one of the highest internet penetration rates and digital literacy levels globally, driven by robust infrastructure and strong government support for digital education.
- **India**: India has seen rapid growth in internet usage, particularly through mobile phones. Programs like Digital India aim to improve digital literacy, though rural areas and certain demographics still face challenges.
- **China**: China has a high internet penetration rate, with extensive government initiatives to promote digital literacy. However, there are significant regional disparities, with rural areas lagging behind urban centers.
- **Japan**: Japan has high digital literacy levels, supported by advanced infrastructure and a strong educational system that integrates digital skills from an early age.

Europe

- **Estonia**: Estonia is a leader in digital literacy and e-governance. The country's focus on digital education and integration of digital services has set a benchmark globally.
- **Germany**: Germany has high internet penetration and digital literacy, supported by comprehensive digital education programs. However, the country continues to address disparities in rural areas.
- **Sweden**: With one of the highest internet penetration rates, Sweden emphasizes digital literacy through its education system and various government initiatives.
- **United Kingdom**: The UK has robust digital literacy programs and high internet penetration, although efforts continue to address regional disparities and ensure inclusivity.

North America

- **United States**: The US has high internet penetration and digital literacy rates, driven by advanced infrastructure and extensive digital education initiatives. However, there are notable disparities among different socioeconomic groups and regions.
- **Canada**: Canada boasts high digital literacy levels, supported by strong education systems and government initiatives. Efforts continue to address access and literacy disparities in remote and indigenous communities.

Latin America and the Caribbean

- **Brazil**: Brazil has seen significant growth in internet usage, particularly through mobile devices. Government programs like the National Broadband Plan aim to improve digital literacy, though challenges remain in rural and low-income areas.
- **Mexico**: Mexico has moderate internet penetration and digital literacy rates, with government initiatives like the National Digital Strategy focusing on improving digital skills across the population.
- **Argentina**: Argentina has made strides in digital literacy through educational programs and increased internet access, although economic challenges impact progress.
- **Chile**: Chile has relatively high internet penetration and digital literacy levels, driven by government initiatives and a strong focus on digital education.

Oceania

- **Australia**: Australia has high internet penetration and digital literacy rates, supported by comprehensive digital education programs and strong government policies. However, efforts continue to address disparities in remote areas.
- **New Zealand**: New Zealand boasts high digital literacy levels, driven by robust infrastructure and a focus on integrating digital skills into the education system.

Conclusion

This chapter has provided an overview of recent statistics on global internet usage, mobile phone penetration, and digital literacy levels. By analyzing significant global trends and disparities, and highlighting countries with notable advancements or challenges, we gain a deeper understanding of the digital landscape. The next chapters will delve into the specific factors shaping digital literacy, including government policies, educational initiatives, and the role of technology in various sectors. Through this comprehensive exploration, we aim to empower readers with the knowledge to navigate and contribute to the digital world effectively.

Chapter 3:

Government Policies on Digital Literacy and Internet Usage

The digital revolution has prompted governments worldwide to implement various initiatives, regulations, and policies aimed at enhancing digital literacy, expanding internet access, and ensuring cybersecurity. These efforts are crucial for fostering inclusive economic growth, social development, and individual empowerment. This chapter explores key government policies across different continents, presents case studies of successful national digital literacy programs, and evaluates the impact of these policies on digital literacy and societal development.

Overview of Government Initiatives, Regulations, and Policies

Governments around the world have recognized the importance of digital literacy and have taken deliberate steps to improve it through various initiatives and policies. Here, we examine notable examples from different continents:

Africa

Kenya: The Digital Literacy Programme (DLP) aims to integrate ICT into primary education by providing digital devices, training teachers, and developing digital content. The initiative has significantly enhanced digital skills among young learners.

South Africa: The National Development Plan 2030 emphasizes the importance of digital literacy and proposes measures to improve ICT infrastructure and digital skills training. The government has also launched the National e-Strategy, which includes digital literacy as a key component.

Asia

India: The Digital India initiative seeks to transform India into a digitally empowered society. Key components include the BharatNet project to provide broadband connectivity to rural areas, the Pradhan Mantri Gramin Digital Saksharta Abhiyan (PMGDISHA) to impart digital literacy to rural citizens, and the National Digital Literacy Mission (NDLM).

Singapore: The Smart Nation initiative focuses on harnessing digital technologies to improve quality of life and business opportunities. It includes programs like the Digital Readiness Blueprint, which outlines strategies to enhance digital literacy and inclusion.

Europe

Estonia: Estonia's e-Estonia initiative is a comprehensive digital strategy that includes e-governance, digital identity, and extensive digital literacy programs. The country's focus on digital education from a young age has made it a global leader in digital literacy.

Germany: The Digital Strategy 2025 outlines Germany's vision for digital transformation, including improving digital skills through education and vocational training. The Digital Pact for Schools provides funding to enhance digital infrastructure and resources in schools.

North America

United States: The National Broadband Plan aims to ensure universal broadband access and promote digital literacy. Initiatives like the ConnectHome program focus on bridging the digital divide in low-income communities, while the E-Rate program provides funding to schools and libraries for internet access and digital resources.

Canada: Canada's Digital Literacy Exchange Program supports non-profit organizations in delivering digital literacy training to marginalized groups. The Innovation and Skills Plan emphasizes digital skills development as a key driver of economic growth.

Latin America and the Caribbean

Brazil: The National Broadband Plan aims to expand internet access across the country, particularly in underserved areas. The Ministry of Education's ProInfo program integrates ICT into education, providing digital devices and training to schools.

Chile: The Digital Agenda 2020 outlines Chile's strategy for digital transformation, including initiatives to enhance digital skills and expand internet access. The government's Enlaces program focuses on integrating ICT into education.

Oceania

Australia: The National Digital Economy Strategy aims to position Australia as a leading digital economy by improving digital skills and expanding broadband access. The Digital

Technologies Hub provides resources for educators to integrate digital literacy into the curriculum.

New Zealand: The Digital Inclusion Blueprint outlines New Zealand's approach to ensuring all citizens have the skills and access needed to participate in the digital world. The Ministry of Education's Digital Technologies curriculum supports digital literacy from an early age.

Case Studies of Successful National Digital Literacy Programs

To illustrate the impact of government policies on digital literacy, we examine successful national programs from various continents:

Africa

Rwanda's Digital Ambassadors Program (DAP): Launched in 2017, this program trains young Rwandans as digital ambassadors who then educate citizens on digital literacy, internet use, and e-services. This initiative has significantly increased digital literacy rates, particularly in rural areas.

Ghana's iBox Initiative: The Ghana Education Service introduced the iBox, a digital platform providing educational content and resources to schools. This program aims to improve digital literacy among students and teachers.

Asia

India's Pradhan Mantri Gramin Digital Saksharta Abhiyan (PMGDISHA): This ambitious program aims to make six crore (60 million) rural households digitally literate. By providing training in digital skills, the initiative has empowered rural citizens to participate in the digital economy.

South Korea's Digital New Deal: Part of the broader Korean New Deal, this initiative focuses on expanding digital infrastructure and promoting digital skills training. South Korea's emphasis on lifelong learning and digital literacy has made it one of the most digitally advanced countries.

Europe

Estonia's e-Estonia Program: Estonia's comprehensive approach to digital governance includes extensive digital literacy initiatives. Programs like ProgeTiiger introduce coding and digital skills to students from a young age, fostering a highly literate digital population.

Finland's Code School Finland: This program provides digital skills and coding education to students of all ages. Finland's national curriculum emphasizes digital literacy, ensuring that all students acquire essential digital competencies.

North America

United States' ConnectHome Initiative: Launched by the Department of Housing and Urban Development (HUD), ConnectHome aims to bridge the digital divide in low-income communities by providing internet access, digital devices, and literacy training. The initiative has reached thousands of households, improving digital literacy and connectivity.

Canada's Digital Literacy Exchange Program (DLEP): Funded by the federal government, DLEP supports non-profit organizations in delivering digital literacy training to underrepresented groups. The program focuses on enhancing digital skills among seniors, low-income individuals, and rural residents.

Latin America and the Caribbean

Brazil's ProInfo Program: This initiative by the Ministry of Education integrates ICT into public schools, providing digital devices, infrastructure, and training to educators and students. ProInfo has significantly improved digital literacy and access to digital resources.

Uruguay's Plan Ceibal: Launched in 2007, Plan Ceibal provides each primary and secondary school student with a laptop and internet access. The program includes digital literacy training for both students and teachers, contributing to higher digital literacy rates and educational outcomes.

Oceania

Australia's National Broadband Network (NBN): The NBN initiative aims to provide high-speed internet access to all Australians, particularly in remote and rural areas. Coupled with digital literacy programs like Be Connected, which supports older Australians in developing digital skills, the NBN has had a substantial impact on digital inclusion.

New Zealand's Digital Technologies Curriculum: Introduced in 2018, this curriculum integrates digital technologies and computational thinking into the education system from an early age. The program aims to ensure all students acquire essential digital skills, preparing them for the digital future.

Evaluation of the Impact of These Policies on Digital Literacy and Societal Development

Government policies and initiatives play a crucial role in shaping digital literacy and its broader societal impacts. Here, we evaluate the effectiveness of these efforts in different regions:

Africa

In Africa, government initiatives have made significant strides in improving digital literacy, particularly in countries like Rwanda and Kenya. Programs like Rwanda's DAP have empowered citizens with digital skills, fostering economic opportunities and social inclusion. However, challenges such as infrastructure deficits and socioeconomic disparities continue to hinder progress.

Asia

Asian countries like South Korea and India have demonstrated the transformative potential of robust digital literacy policies. South Korea's Digital New Deal and India's PMGDISHA have not only enhanced digital skills but also contributed to economic growth and social empowerment. Nonetheless, regional disparities within countries remain a concern.

Europe

European countries, notably Estonia and Finland, have set benchmarks in digital literacy through comprehensive policies and education reforms. Estonia's e-Estonia program and Finland's coding initiatives have fostered a digitally literate populace, driving innovation and economic competitiveness. The success of these programs highlights the importance of early and continuous digital education.

North America

In North America, initiatives like the United States' ConnectHome and Canada's DLEP have effectively addressed digital divides in marginalized communities. These programs have improved digital literacy, facilitating better access to education, employment, and social services. However, ongoing efforts are needed to address disparities in remote and rural areas.

Latin America and the Caribbean

Programs like Brazil's ProInfo and Uruguay's Plan Ceibal have significantly enhanced digital literacy in Latin America. These initiatives have improved educational outcomes and digital skills, contributing to social and economic development. Challenges such as infrastructure gaps and economic instability, however, continue to affect the region's digital progress.

Oceania

In Oceania, Australia's NBN and New Zealand's Digital Technologies Curriculum have had a profound impact on digital literacy and inclusion. These initiatives have ensured widespread access to digital resources and education, promoting social inclusion and economic development. The success of these programs underscores the importance of combining infrastructure development with digital literacy training.

Conclusion

Government policies and initiatives are pivotal in advancing digital literacy and ensuring equitable access to the digital world. By examining various successful programs across continents, this chapter has highlighted the critical role of strategic policy-making in fostering digital skills and societal development. The next chapters will delve deeper into specific aspects of digital literacy, including its integration into education, the digital economy, and the implications for cybersecurity and social media. Through this comprehensive exploration, we aim to equip readers with a thorough understanding of the global landscape of digital literacy.

Chapter 4:

Digital Literacy in Education

In today's rapidly evolving digital age, education systems worldwide are increasingly integrating digital tools and internet resources into their curricula to enhance learning and prepare students for the future. This chapter explores how schools and universities across different continents are embracing digital literacy, presents success stories and challenges in enhancing education through digital means, and examines the crucial role of digital literacy in remote learning, particularly in the context of the COVID-19 pandemic.

How Schools and Universities Globally are Integrating Digital Tools and Internet Resources into their Curricula

Africa

South Africa: University of Johannesburg (UJ) The University of Johannesburg is a pioneer in integrating digital tools within its curriculum. UJ employs blended learning strategies, utilizing platforms like Blackboard to deliver course content, facilitate communication, and engage students. The university also offers extensive online resources and training for both students and faculty to enhance digital literacy.

Kenya: Aga Khan Academy, Mombasa The Aga Khan Academy in Mombasa integrates digital literacy into its International Baccalaureate (IB) curriculum. The school uses digital tools for collaborative projects, research, and presentations, ensuring students are proficient in using technology to support their learning.

Asia

Singapore: Nanyang Technological University (NTU) NTU is at the forefront of digital integration in education. It employs a range of digital tools, such as the NTULearn platform, which supports online lectures, tutorials, and assessments. NTU also emphasizes digital skills across various disciplines, preparing students for the demands of the digital economy.

South Korea: Korea Advanced Institute of Science and Technology (KAIST) KAIST utilizes advanced digital technologies and online platforms to enhance education. The university's Smart Learning System (SLS) offers personalized learning experiences, integrating AI and big data to tailor content to individual students' needs.

Europe

Estonia: Tallinn University Tallinn University is renowned for its digital literacy initiatives. The university incorporates digital tools extensively in its curriculum, offering courses on digital competencies, e-governance, and cybersecurity. Tallinn University also promotes the use of digital portfolios to track and showcase students' progress.

Finland: Helsinki University Helsinki University integrates digital tools through its DigiCampus initiative, which provides a comprehensive online learning environment. The university focuses on developing digital competencies among students and faculty, offering courses and resources on digital pedagogy and ICT skills.

North America

United States: Massachusetts Institute of Technology (MIT) MIT leads the way in digital integration with its MITx platform, part of the edX consortium, offering numerous online courses and resources. The university emphasizes the development of digital skills through hands-on projects, coding bootcamps, and digital labs.

Canada: University of British Columbia (UBC) UBC has implemented extensive digital literacy programs, integrating tools like Canvas for online learning and collaboration. The university offers workshops and resources to enhance digital skills among students and faculty, supporting a comprehensive digital learning environment.

Latin America and the Caribbean

Brazil: University of São Paulo (USP) USP incorporates digital tools across its curriculum, using platforms like Moodle to facilitate online learning. The university also offers digital literacy courses and workshops, ensuring students are equipped with the necessary skills to thrive in a digital world.

Chile: Pontifical Catholic University of Chile This university leverages digital technologies to support education, using platforms like UC Online for course delivery and collaboration. The university emphasizes digital competencies, offering courses on digital tools, online research methods, and e-learning strategies.

Oceania

Australia: University of Melbourne The University of Melbourne integrates digital tools extensively within its curriculum, using platforms like LMS (Learning Management System) for online course delivery and interaction. The university offers digital literacy programs, focusing on developing ICT skills and digital competencies among students.

New Zealand: University of Auckland The University of Auckland employs digital tools such as Canvas to support online learning and collaboration. The university provides comprehensive digital literacy training, ensuring students and faculty are proficient in using digital technologies for educational purposes.

Success Stories and Challenges in Enhancing Education through Digital Means

Success Stories

Estonia: ProgeTiiger Program Estonia's ProgeTiiger program has been highly successful in integrating coding and digital skills into the national curriculum. Starting from primary education, students learn programming and digital literacy, which has led to Estonia being recognized as a leader in digital education.

India: Diksha Platform India's Diksha platform offers teachers, students, and parents access to a wide range of digital resources. It has been particularly successful in providing educational content in multiple languages, reaching millions of students across the country and enhancing digital literacy at all levels.

United States: Khan Academy Khan Academy is a notable example of enhancing education through digital means. This non-profit organization provides free online courses, tutorials, and practice exercises across various subjects. It has empowered millions of learners globally, improving digital literacy and access to quality education.

Challenges

Infrastructure Limitations In many regions, particularly in developing countries, inadequate infrastructure poses a significant challenge. Limited access to high-speed internet, digital devices, and reliable electricity hampers the effective integration of digital tools in education.

Digital Divide The digital divide remains a major challenge, with disparities in digital literacy and access to technology between urban and rural areas, and among different socioeconomic groups. This divide exacerbates educational inequalities and hinders the widespread adoption of digital tools.

Teacher Training Effective integration of digital tools requires adequately trained teachers. In many cases, educators lack the necessary digital skills and confidence to effectively utilize technology in their teaching, which impedes the successful implementation of digital literacy programs.

Role of Digital Literacy in Remote Learning, Particularly Highlighted by the COVID-19 Pandemic

The COVID-19 pandemic has underscored the critical role of digital literacy in remote learning. As schools and universities worldwide shifted to online education, digital literacy became essential for both students and educators to navigate and succeed in this new learning environment.

Rapid Transition to Online Learning

Global Shift to Online Platforms The pandemic forced educational institutions globally to transition to online platforms. Universities like Harvard and Stanford quickly moved their courses online, leveraging platforms such as Zoom, Canvas, and Google Classroom to continue education without interruption.

Innovative Solutions Countries like China implemented innovative solutions to support remote learning. The Ministry of Education launched the "Disrupted Classes, Undisrupted Learning" initiative, providing online resources and broadcasts of educational content to millions of students.

Challenges in Remote Learning

Access and Equity The abrupt shift to remote learning highlighted significant disparities in access to digital devices and reliable internet. Students from low-income families and rural areas faced considerable challenges in participating in online education, exacerbating educational inequities.

Digital Skills Gap The pandemic revealed a digital skills gap among both students and educators. Many struggled with using online platforms and digital tools effectively, underscoring the need for comprehensive digital literacy training to support remote learning.

Success Stories

Italy: School on the Cloud Italy's "School on the Cloud" initiative successfully transitioned to online education during the pandemic. The program provided teachers with training and resources to deliver effective online lessons, ensuring continuity of education despite the lockdown.

Kenya: Eneza Education Eneza Education, a mobile learning platform, played a crucial role in supporting remote learning during the pandemic. By providing educational content via SMS and mobile apps, Eneza reached millions of students, particularly in underserved areas, enhancing digital literacy and access to education.

Conclusion

Digital literacy is fundamental to modern education, enabling schools and universities to integrate digital tools and internet resources effectively into their curricula. This chapter has explored various global initiatives, success stories, and challenges in enhancing education through digital means. The COVID-19 pandemic has further highlighted the critical role of digital literacy in remote learning, underscoring the need for continued investment in digital infrastructure, training, and resources. As we move forward, it is imperative to address the digital divide and ensure that all students and educators are equipped with the necessary digital skills to thrive in the digital age.

Chapter 5:

Remote Work and the Digital Economy

The landscape of work has undergone a dramatic transformation in recent years, with the adoption of remote work accelerating globally due to the COVID-19 pandemic. This chapter delves into the worldwide shift towards remote work, the pivotal role of digital literacy in enabling this transition, and the broader implications for the global job market. It also explores the concept of digital nomadism and anticipates the future of work in a digital economy.

Exploration of the Adoption of Remote Work Globally, Accelerated by the COVID-19 Pandemic

Global Shift to Remote Work

The COVID-19 pandemic acted as a catalyst for remote work, forcing businesses and organizations across the world to adopt work-from-home models. Before the pandemic, remote work was gaining traction, but its adoption was relatively gradual. The pandemic, however, accelerated this trend exponentially.

- **United States**: According to a report by FlexJobs and Global Workplace Analytics, remote work in the U.S. increased by 159% between 2005 and 2017. By mid-2020, nearly 42% of the U.S. labor force was working remotely full-time .

- **Europe**: The European Commission reported that remote work in the EU rose from 5% before the pandemic to around 40% during the first lockdowns in 2020 .
- **Asia**: In Japan, remote work adoption increased significantly, with a survey by Persol Research and Consulting showing that 27.9% of companies had introduced telecommuting by mid-2020, compared to just 13.2% before the pandemic.
- **Africa**: While remote work was less prevalent, countries like South Africa saw substantial increases. A study by the International Labour Organization (ILO) indicated that the share of remote workers in South Africa rose from 10% to 24% during the pandemic.

Government Policies Influenced by Remote Work Trends

Governments worldwide have responded to the rise in remote work with various policies and initiatives to support this transition:

- **United Kingdom**: The UK government introduced the Coronavirus Job Retention Scheme, which included support for remote working infrastructure and flexible working arrangements.
- **Singapore**: The Singaporean government launched the SGUnited Jobs and Skills Package, which provides support for digital tools and remote working capabilities for businesses.
- **India**: The Indian government implemented guidelines for remote work in the IT sector, providing tax incentives and infrastructure support to facilitate the shift.

The Role of Digital Literacy in Enabling Remote Work and Its Impact on the Global Job Market

Importance of Digital Literacy

Digital literacy has become a cornerstone of remote work, enabling individuals to navigate and utilize digital tools effectively. Key components of digital literacy in the context of remote work include proficiency in communication platforms (e.g., Zoom, Microsoft Teams), project management tools (e.g., Asana, Trello), and collaboration software (e.g., Google Workspace, Slack).

- **Proficiency in Communication Platforms**: Tools like Zoom and Microsoft Teams have become essential for virtual meetings, webinars, and online collaboration. These platforms require users to understand how to set up meetings, share screens, and use various interactive features.
- **Project Management Tools**: Asana and Trello help remote teams manage projects, track progress, and collaborate efficiently. Understanding how to use these tools is crucial for maintaining productivity in a remote work environment.
- **Collaboration Software**: Google Workspace and Slack facilitate real-time collaboration, document sharing, and team communication. Mastery of these tools is vital for seamless remote work operations.

Impact on the Global Job Market

The rise of remote work has had profound effects on the global job market, reshaping employment opportunities and workforce dynamics:

- **Increased Demand for Digital Skills**: The demand for digital skills has surged, with roles in IT, digital marketing, and data analysis becoming increasingly sought after. According to LinkedIn's 2020 Jobs on the Rise report, remote job postings for digital content creators, software developers, and data scientists increased by over 50% during the pandemic.
- **Geographical Flexibility**: Remote work has decoupled jobs from geographic locations, allowing companies to hire talent from anywhere in the world. This has opened up opportunities for workers in regions with fewer local job prospects to access global markets.
- **Shift in Work-Life Balance**: Remote work has offered greater flexibility, enabling employees to achieve a better work-life balance. However, it has also blurred the boundaries between work and personal life, leading to challenges in managing work hours and maintaining mental well-being.

Websites for Remote Work and In-Demand Skills

There are numerous platforms and websites that connect remote workers with job opportunities. Some of the most popular include:

- **Upwork**: A global freelancing platform that connects businesses with remote professionals in various fields such as writing, graphic design, and software development.
- **Remote.co**: A resource for remote job listings across different industries, providing advice and insights on remote work.
- **We Work Remotely**: A job board specifically for remote job opportunities, catering to a wide range of professions.
- **FlexJobs**: A platform that specializes in flexible and remote job listings, offering opportunities in over 50 career categories.

In-demand skills for remote work include:

- **Digital Marketing**: Skills in SEO, social media management, and content creation are highly sought after.
- **Software Development**: Proficiency in programming languages such as Python, JavaScript, and Java remains crucial.
- **Data Analysis**: The ability to analyze and interpret data using tools like Excel, SQL, and Tableau is essential.
- **Project Management**: Expertise in managing projects using tools like Asana, Trello, and Jira is valuable.

- **Customer Support**: Skills in handling customer inquiries and support through digital platforms are in high demand.

Discussion on Digital Nomadism and the Future of Work

Digital Nomadism

Digital nomadism, the practice of working remotely from various locations around the world, has gained popularity as remote work has become more widespread. Digital nomads leverage technology to maintain their careers while exploring new places and cultures.

- **Popular Destinations**: Cities like Bali, Chiang Mai, and Lisbon have become hubs for digital nomads due to their affordable living costs, vibrant expat communities, and reliable internet infrastructure.
- **Challenges and Considerations**: While digital nomadism offers flexibility and adventure, it also presents challenges such as visa regulations, access to healthcare, and maintaining productivity while traveling.

The Future of Work

The future of work is likely to be characterized by increased flexibility, digital integration, and a focus on skills over location. Key trends shaping the future of work include:

- **Hybrid Work Models**: Many organizations are adopting hybrid work models, combining remote and in-office work to offer flexibility while maintaining collaboration and company culture.
- **Automation and AI**: Advances in automation and artificial intelligence are transforming job roles and creating new opportunities in tech-driven fields.
- **Continuous Learning**: The rapid pace of technological change necessitates continuous learning and upskilling to remain competitive in the job market.

Conclusion

The adoption of remote work has transformed the global job market, emphasizing the importance of digital literacy in navigating this new landscape. As digital nomadism becomes more popular and the future of work evolves, individuals and organizations must adapt to the changing dynamics of the digital economy. By embracing digital tools, enhancing digital skills, and fostering a culture of continuous learning, we can harness the opportunities of remote work and shape a more flexible, inclusive, and productive future.

Chapter 6:

The Role of Social Media

In the modern digital landscape, social media platforms have become integral to everyday life, influencing how we communicate, share information, engage in civic activities, and form public opinion. This chapter explores the global popularity and impact of social media, examines its multifaceted uses, and analyzes its influence on public opinion, culture, and politics.

Analysis of the Global Popularity and Impact of Social Media Platforms

Global Reach and Popularity

Social media platforms have experienced exponential growth over the past decade, connecting billions of people across the globe. As of 2023:

- **Facebook**: With over 2.9 billion monthly active users, Facebook remains the largest social media platform globally. Its widespread adoption spans all continents, with significant user bases in North America, Asia, and Africa.
- **YouTube**: With 2.5 billion users, YouTube is a leading platform for video content, popular across diverse age groups and regions.

- **WhatsApp**: This messaging app boasts over 2 billion users worldwide, particularly popular in countries like India, Brazil, and South Africa.
- **Instagram**: Known for its visual content, Instagram has over 2 billion users, with strong followings in North America, Europe, and increasingly in Asia.
- **TikTok**: A newer entrant, TikTok has rapidly gained popularity, especially among younger users, with 1 billion users globally, including significant growth in the Americas, Europe, and Southeast Asia.

Regional Trends and Disparities

- **North America**: Social media usage is high, with platforms like Facebook, Instagram, and Twitter dominating. The region also sees significant use of LinkedIn for professional networking.
- **Europe**: Similar trends to North America, with additional popularity for regional platforms like VKontakte in Eastern Europe and Russia.
- **Asia**: The largest market for social media users, driven by populous countries like India and China. WeChat is predominant in China, while platforms like TikTok, WhatsApp, and Instagram lead in other parts of Asia.
- **Africa**: Rapid growth in social media usage, with WhatsApp and Facebook leading. The rise in mobile phone usage has significantly contributed to this trend.
- **Latin America**: High engagement on Facebook, WhatsApp, and Instagram. Social media is a primary source of information and communication in many countries.

- **Oceania**: High internet penetration and social media usage, similar to North America and Europe, with a strong presence on Facebook and Instagram.

How Social Media Is Used for Communication, Information Dissemination, Civic Engagement, and Activism

Communication

Social media has revolutionized communication, allowing instantaneous interaction across vast distances. Platforms like Facebook, WhatsApp, and Instagram enable users to stay connected with friends and family, share updates, and engage in real-time conversations. The rise of video calls and live streaming has further enriched these interactions.

Information Dissemination

Social media serves as a critical channel for news and information dissemination:

- **Twitter**: Known for real-time updates, Twitter is widely used by journalists, politicians, and public figures to share news and opinions.
- **Facebook and YouTube**: These platforms host news outlets and independent content creators, providing a wide range of perspectives and information.
- **TikTok**: Emerging as a source of news, especially for younger audiences, with creators and organizations using short videos to inform and educate.

Civic Engagement and Activism

Social media has become a powerful tool for civic engagement and activism, enabling users to organize, mobilize, and advocate for causes:

- **Arab Spring**: In the early 2010s, social media played a crucial role in organizing protests and disseminating information during the Arab Spring, demonstrating its potential for political mobilization.
- **#BlackLivesMatter**: The movement gained global traction through platforms like Twitter, Instagram, and Facebook, highlighting issues of racial injustice and police brutality.
- **#MeToo**: This movement against sexual harassment and assault spread virally on social media, empowering individuals to share their stories and demand change.

Examples from Each Continent

- **North America**: The use of social media for political campaigns and civic engagement is prominent. Platforms like Twitter and Facebook are integral to political discourse and grassroots organizing.
- **Europe**: Social media has been pivotal in movements like the Yellow Vests in France and climate activism led by Greta Thunberg across Europe.
- **Asia**: In Hong Kong, social media was used extensively to organize pro-democracy protests and communicate with the international community.
- **Africa**: In Nigeria, the #EndSARS movement leveraged social media to protest against police brutality, gaining international support and attention.

- **Latin America**: In Chile, social media played a crucial role in organizing protests against economic inequality and advocating for constitutional reforms.
- **Oceania**: Social media is used for environmental activism, such as campaigns against deforestation and climate change in Australia and New Zealand.

The Influence of Social Media on Public Opinion, Culture, and Politics

Shaping Public Opinion

Social media platforms are influential in shaping public opinion through the dissemination of information, user interactions, and algorithm-driven content:

- **Echo Chambers and Filter Bubbles**: Algorithms that personalize content can create echo chambers, where users are exposed primarily to information that reinforces their existing beliefs, potentially polarizing public opinion.
- **Viral Content**: The rapid spread of viral content can shape public discourse and bring attention to specific issues, influencing how people perceive events and policies.

Cultural Influence

Social media influences culture by facilitating the exchange of ideas, trends, and cultural practices:

- **Globalization of Culture**: Platforms like YouTube and Instagram enable the global sharing of music, fashion, and art, contributing to a more interconnected cultural landscape.
- **Memes and Internet Culture**: Social media has given rise to internet culture, with memes becoming a significant aspect of contemporary cultural expression.

Political Impact

The political impact of social media is profound, affecting how campaigns are run, how political messages are communicated, and how public engagement is managed:

- **Campaign Strategies**: Political campaigns utilize social media for targeted advertising, voter engagement, and mobilizing support. Barack Obama's 2008 campaign is often cited as a pioneering use of social media in politics.
- **Disinformation and Misinformation**: The spread of false information on social media can influence elections and political opinions, posing challenges for maintaining informed and democratic societies.
- **Regulation and Policy**: Governments and regulatory bodies are increasingly focusing on the role of social media in politics, with initiatives to address issues like data privacy, election interference, and content moderation.

Conclusion

Social media has become a cornerstone of modern communication, information dissemination, civic engagement, and cultural exchange. Its global reach and influence on public opinion, culture, and politics are undeniable. As social media continues to evolve, understanding its dynamics and impacts will be crucial for navigating the digital age and leveraging its potential for positive societal change.

Chapter 7:

E-Commerce and Digital Literacy

The advent and rapid growth of e-commerce have transformed the global retail landscape, impacting traditional retail and creating new opportunities and challenges for consumers and entrepreneurs alike. This chapter explores the worldwide growth of e-commerce, the digital skills necessary for effective participation, and the challenges and opportunities for enhancing digital literacy in the context of online shopping and digital marketplaces.

Growth of E-Commerce Worldwide and Its Impact on Traditional Retail

Global Expansion of E-Commerce

E-commerce has experienced exponential growth globally, driven by increased internet penetration, advances in technology, and changes in consumer behavior. As of 2023, global e-commerce sales are estimated to reach $5.5 trillion, with projections suggesting further growth in the coming years. This boom is evident across all continents:

- **North America**: The United States remains a leader in e-commerce, with giants like Amazon and eBay dominating the market. Canada also shows significant growth, with major retailers enhancing their online presence.
- **Europe**: The e-commerce market in Europe is thriving, with the UK, Germany, and France being the top players. The European Union's Digital Single Market

strategy aims to harmonize regulations and boost cross-border e-commerce.

- **Asia**: China is the largest e-commerce market globally, driven by platforms like Alibaba and JD.com. India is also seeing rapid growth, with increased internet access and mobile phone usage fueling online shopping.
- **Africa**: Although still emerging, e-commerce in Africa is growing, with companies like Jumia leading the charge. Mobile money services such as M-Pesa in Kenya are facilitating online transactions.
- **Latin America**: Brazil and Mexico are the leading e-commerce markets in the region, with a burgeoning middle class and improved internet infrastructure contributing to growth.
- **Oceania**: Australia and New Zealand have well-developed e-commerce markets, with high internet penetration and consumer trust in online shopping.

Impact on Traditional Retail

The rise of e-commerce has significantly impacted traditional retail, leading to both challenges and opportunities:

- **Shift in Consumer Behavior**: Consumers increasingly prefer the convenience of online shopping, which offers a wider range of products, competitive prices, and home delivery.
- **Brick-and-Mortar Stores**: Traditional retailers are adapting by developing online platforms, integrating omnichannel strategies, and enhancing in-store experiences to attract customers.

- **Economic Implications**: The growth of e-commerce has led to job creation in logistics, warehousing, and technology sectors, but also posed challenges for retail jobs and small businesses struggling to compete online.

Digital Skills Required for Participating in E-Commerce, Both as Consumers and Entrepreneurs

Essential Digital Skills for Consumers

To effectively participate in e-commerce, consumers need a range of digital skills, including:

- **Online Shopping Competency**: Understanding how to navigate e-commerce platforms, search for products, compare prices, and read reviews.
- **Digital Payment Literacy**: Familiarity with various online payment methods, including credit/debit cards, mobile wallets, and cryptocurrencies.
- **Cybersecurity Awareness**: Knowledge of how to protect personal information, recognize phishing scams, and ensure safe transactions.

Key Digital Skills for Entrepreneurs

Entrepreneurs entering the e-commerce space need to develop specific digital competencies to succeed:

- **Website Development and Management**: Skills in creating and maintaining user-friendly e-commerce websites using platforms like Shopify, WooCommerce, or custom solutions.

- **Digital Marketing**: Proficiency in search engine optimization (SEO), social media marketing, email marketing, and online advertising to attract and retain customers.
- **Data Analytics**: Ability to analyze consumer behavior, sales trends, and website performance to make data-driven decisions.
- **Inventory and Supply Chain Management**: Knowledge of managing inventory, logistics, and supply chains to ensure timely delivery and customer satisfaction.

Examples from Different Continents

- **North America**: Entrepreneurs leverage platforms like Shopify (Canada) to set up and manage online stores efficiently. Digital marketing through social media and search engines is critical for reaching consumers.
- **Europe**: Businesses use multi-lingual websites and cross-border shipping solutions to tap into the diverse European market. E-commerce entrepreneurs often benefit from EU regulations that facilitate online trade.
- **Asia**: In China, platforms like Alibaba provide comprehensive tools for entrepreneurs, including access to a vast consumer base and advanced logistics networks. India sees a rise in small businesses using platforms like Flipkart and Amazon India.
- **Africa**: Digital skills training programs, such as those offered by Jumia, help local entrepreneurs enter the e-commerce market. Mobile money platforms enable secure transactions for consumers without traditional banking access.
- **Latin America**: Marketplaces like MercadoLibre provide tools and support for local businesses to go

online. Entrepreneurs need skills in digital marketing and customer service to succeed.

- **Oceania**: In Australia and New Zealand, businesses focus on high-quality websites and digital marketing strategies to compete in a well-developed e-commerce market.

Challenges and Opportunities for Enhancing Digital Literacy in the Context of Online Shopping and Digital Marketplaces

Challenges

Several challenges impede the enhancement of digital literacy for e-commerce:

- **Access to Technology**: Limited internet access and technology infrastructure in rural and underserved areas.
- **Cybersecurity Concerns**: High rates of cybercrime and a lack of awareness about online security practices.
- **Economic Barriers**: Financial constraints preventing individuals and businesses from investing in the necessary technology and skills training.
- **Cultural and Language Barriers**: Diverse languages and cultural practices affecting the adoption and usability of e-commerce platforms.

Opportunities

Despite these challenges, there are numerous opportunities to enhance digital literacy in e-commerce:

- **Educational Programs**: Government and private sector initiatives offering digital skills training and e-commerce education. For instance, programs like Google's Digital Garage provide free online courses on digital marketing and e-commerce.
- **Public-Private Partnerships**: Collaborations between governments, tech companies, and educational institutions to bridge the digital divide. Examples include the African Development Bank's Coding for Employment program.
- **Innovation and Technology**: Advancements in technology, such as mobile payment solutions and AI-driven customer service, making e-commerce more accessible and efficient.
- **Community Support and Networks**: Online communities and support networks that provide resources, advice, and mentorship for aspiring e-commerce entrepreneurs.

Conclusion

The growth of e-commerce has reshaped the global retail landscape, offering immense opportunities for consumers and entrepreneurs who possess the necessary digital skills. Enhancing digital literacy in the context of e-commerce is essential for maximizing these opportunities and addressing the challenges posed by this dynamic market. By fostering digital competencies and leveraging innovative solutions, individuals and businesses worldwide can fully participate in and benefit from the burgeoning digital economy.

Chapter 8:

Digital Assets and Cybersecurity

Explanation of Digital Assets and Their Relevance to Individuals and Businesses Globally

In the rapidly evolving digital economy, digital assets have emerged as a significant and transformative force. Digital assets encompass a variety of forms, including cryptocurrencies, non-fungible tokens (NFTs), and digital securities. These assets are underpinned by blockchain technology, which ensures transparency, security, and decentralization.

Cryptocurrencies

Cryptocurrencies, such as Bitcoin and Ethereum, are decentralized digital currencies that use cryptographic techniques to secure transactions. Bitcoin, the first and most well-known cryptocurrency, was introduced in 2009 by an anonymous entity known as Satoshi Nakamoto. Bitcoin operates on a decentralized network, meaning it is not controlled by any government or financial institution. This decentralized nature offers users a sense of financial sovereignty and security against inflation and traditional banking failures.

Individuals and businesses globally have found numerous ways to monetize and earn from cryptocurrencies. For instance:

- **Mining**: This process involves using powerful computers to solve complex mathematical problems that validate transactions on the blockchain. Successful miners are rewarded with newly minted coins. Countries like China (before regulatory crackdowns), Russia, and Canada have been hotspots for mining due to their access to cheap electricity and suitable climates.
- **Trading and Investing**: Cryptocurrency exchanges, such as Coinbase and Binance, allow users to buy, sell, and trade a wide variety of digital currencies. Investors from the United States, Japan, and South Korea, among others, engage in this market, seeking to capitalize on the volatility and potential high returns of cryptocurrencies.
- **Payments and Remittances**: Cryptocurrencies are increasingly being used for payments and remittances. In countries with unstable currencies, like Venezuela and Zimbabwe, Bitcoin and other cryptocurrencies offer an alternative means of preserving wealth and facilitating cross-border transactions without exorbitant fees.

Non-Fungible Tokens (NFTs)

NFTs are unique digital assets that represent ownership of a specific item or piece of content, such as art, music, or virtual real estate. Unlike cryptocurrencies, NFTs are indivisible and unique, making them ideal for certifying authenticity and ownership.

The NFT market has seen explosive growth, with artists, musicians, and creators from around the world capitalizing on this new revenue stream. Notable examples include:

- **Art and Collectibles**: Digital artists like Beeple have sold NFTs of their work for millions of dollars. In March 2021, Beeple's digital artwork "Everydays: The First 5000 Days" sold for $69 million at Christie's auction house, highlighting the substantial market for digital art.
- **Music**: Musicians such as Kings of Leon and Grimes have released music and exclusive content as NFTs, generating significant income. These NFTs often include additional perks like concert tickets and backstage passes.
- **Virtual Real Estate**: Platforms like Decentraland and The Sandbox allow users to buy, sell, and develop virtual land parcels. Investors and developers in the United States, Europe, and Asia are actively participating in these virtual real estate markets, creating immersive digital experiences and generating income through virtual commerce and advertising.

Digital Securities

Digital securities, or security tokens, represent traditional financial assets like stocks, bonds, or real estate but are issued and traded on a blockchain. This innovation brings greater efficiency, transparency, and accessibility to the securities market.

Examples of digital securities usage include:

- **Fractional Ownership**: By tokenizing real estate or other valuable assets, individuals can purchase fractional ownership, making it easier to invest in high-value assets. Companies in the United States and Europe are pioneering this approach, allowing broader participation in lucrative markets.

- **Efficient Trading**: Digital securities can be traded more efficiently and with lower fees compared to traditional securities, making markets more accessible to small investors globally.

Overview of Digital Asset Management and Security Practices

Managing digital assets requires a comprehensive understanding of the associated risks and the implementation of robust security practices.

Digital Wallets

Digital wallets are essential tools for storing, sending, and receiving digital assets. There are two main types of wallets:

- **Hot Wallets**: These are connected to the internet and provide easy access for transactions. Examples include software wallets like MetaMask and mobile wallets such as Trust Wallet. While convenient, hot wallets are more vulnerable to hacking and cyberattacks.
- **Cold Wallets**: These are offline storage options, such as hardware wallets (e.g., Ledger and Trezor) and paper wallets. Cold wallets offer enhanced security by keeping the private keys offline, reducing the risk of online attacks.

Security Practices

To protect digital assets, users should adopt best security practices, including:

- **Strong Passwords and Two-Factor Authentication (2FA)**: Using complex passwords and enabling 2FA adds an extra layer of security, making unauthorized access more difficult.
- **Regular Software Updates**: Keeping wallets and related software up to date helps protect against vulnerabilities and exploits.
- **Backup and Recovery**: Regularly backing up wallet data and securing recovery phrases ensures that users can restore their assets in case of loss or hardware failure.
- **Education and Vigilance**: Staying informed about the latest security threats and scams is crucial. Users should be wary of phishing attacks, fake websites, and unsolicited messages.

Institutional Security Measures

For businesses and institutions dealing with digital assets, more advanced security measures are necessary:

- **Multi-Signature Wallets**: These wallets require multiple private keys to authorize a transaction, reducing the risk of a single point of failure. Companies like BitGo and Coinbase Custody offer multi-signature solutions for institutional clients.
- **Custodial Services**: Professional custodians provide secure storage solutions for digital assets. These services often include insurance coverage and

advanced security protocols. Examples include Fidelity Digital Assets and Gemini Custody.

- **Regulatory Compliance**: Ensuring compliance with local and international regulations helps protect businesses from legal risks and enhances trust among customers and partners. Regulatory frameworks for digital assets are evolving, with countries like the United States, Singapore, and Switzerland taking the lead in establishing clear guidelines.

The Role of Digital Literacy in Protecting Against Cyber Threats and Ensuring Safe Online Transactions

Digital literacy plays a critical role in safeguarding individuals and businesses against cyber threats and ensuring secure online transactions.

Understanding Cyber Threats

Digital literacy involves recognizing and understanding various cyber threats, such as:

- **Phishing**: Fraudulent attempts to obtain sensitive information by pretending to be a trustworthy entity. Digital literacy helps users identify suspicious emails and websites, reducing the risk of falling victim to phishing attacks.
- **Malware**: Malicious software designed to disrupt, damage, or gain unauthorized access to computer systems. Educated users are more likely to recognize and avoid downloading or executing suspicious files.

- **Ransomware**: A type of malware that encrypts a user's data and demands payment for its release. Understanding how ransomware works and how to prevent it (e.g., through regular backups and avoiding suspicious links) is crucial for digital safety.

Safe Online Transactions

Ensuring secure online transactions requires a combination of digital literacy and practical security measures:

- **Verifying Authenticity**: Digital literacy enables users to verify the authenticity of websites and digital platforms before conducting transactions. This includes checking URLs, looking for HTTPS encryption, and researching the platform's reputation.
- **Secure Payment Methods**: Using secure payment methods, such as credit cards with fraud protection or reputable payment services like PayPal, adds an extra layer of security. Cryptocurrencies can also be used, but users must ensure they are familiar with the process and risks involved.
- **Privacy Protection**: Digital literacy helps users understand the importance of protecting personal information and being cautious about sharing sensitive data online.

Educating and Empowering Users

Enhancing digital literacy across different demographics is essential for creating a secure digital environment. This can be achieved through:

- **Educational Programs**: Schools, universities, and community organizations can offer courses and workshops on digital literacy, cybersecurity, and safe online practices. Governments and private institutions in countries like Estonia, Finland, and Singapore have implemented successful digital literacy programs.
- **Public Awareness Campaigns**: Governments and NGOs can run awareness campaigns to educate the public about common cyber threats and safe online behaviors. Campaigns like "Stop.Think.Connect." in the United States aim to promote cybersecurity awareness among internet users.
- **Industry Collaboration**: Collaboration between tech companies, cybersecurity firms, and financial institutions can lead to the development of better tools and resources for enhancing digital literacy and security.

Conclusion

Digital assets are reshaping the global economic landscape, offering new opportunities for individuals and businesses. However, with these opportunities come significant risks that require robust digital literacy and security practices. By understanding digital assets, managing them securely, and staying informed about cyber threats, individuals and businesses can navigate the digital world confidently and responsibly.

Chapter 9:

Safe Internet Usage: Addressing Risks

In the age of ubiquitous digital connectivity, safe internet usage has become a critical aspect of digital literacy. As individuals and societies become more reliant on the internet for work, education, social interaction, and entertainment, the associated risks must be thoroughly understood and addressed. This chapter delves into the various dimensions of safe internet usage, examining the risks of internet addiction, the mental health consequences, strategies to mitigate these risks, and the broader issues of online safety, such as cyberbullying, privacy concerns, and data breaches. Additionally, we will explore global initiatives aimed at promoting safe and responsible internet usage.

Risks of Internet Addiction, Its Consequences on Mental Health, and Strategies to Mitigate These Risks

Understanding Internet Addiction

Internet addiction, often referred to as problematic internet use or compulsive internet use, is characterized by excessive or poorly controlled preoccupations, urges, or behaviors regarding computer use and internet access that lead to impairment or distress. This phenomenon has become increasingly prevalent with the rise of social media, online gaming, and streaming services.

Consequences on Mental Health

The consequences of internet addiction on mental health are multifaceted and significant:

- **Emotional Distress**: Excessive internet use can lead to feelings of anxiety, depression, and loneliness. Studies have shown that individuals who spend more time on social media platforms are more likely to experience symptoms of depression and anxiety due to factors such as cyberbullying, social comparison, and the pressure to present a perfect online persona.
- **Cognitive Impairments**: Overuse of the internet can result in cognitive impairments, including difficulties with attention, memory, and decision-making. The constant influx of information and the habit of multitasking can overwhelm the brain, reducing its ability to focus and process information effectively.
- **Physical Health Issues**: Prolonged periods of screen time are associated with various physical health problems, such as eye strain, poor posture, and sleep disturbances. These physical ailments can exacerbate mental health issues, creating a vicious cycle.

Strategies to Mitigate Internet Addiction

Mitigating the risks of internet addiction involves a combination of personal strategies and broader societal interventions:

- **Setting Boundaries**: Individuals can benefit from setting clear boundaries on their internet usage, such as designated times for checking social media or playing games. Using tools like screen time monitors and app usage limits can help in maintaining these boundaries.

- **Promoting Offline Activities**: Encouraging engagement in offline activities, such as physical exercise, hobbies, and face-to-face social interactions, can help balance internet use. Schools, workplaces, and community organizations can play a role by providing opportunities for offline engagement.
- **Mental Health Support**: Access to mental health resources, such as counseling and therapy, can support individuals struggling with internet addiction. Cognitive-behavioral therapy (CBT) has been shown to be particularly effective in addressing addictive behaviors.
- **Educational Programs**: Governments and NGOs can implement educational programs that raise awareness about the risks of internet addiction and promote healthy internet habits. For example, South Korea has established the "Internet Rescue School," a boot camp for young people to help them overcome internet addiction through a structured program that includes physical activities, counseling, and education on balanced internet use.

Examination of Online Safety Issues

Cyberbullying

Cyberbullying involves the use of digital platforms to harass, threaten, or humiliate individuals. It can occur through social media, messaging apps, gaming platforms, and other online channels. The impacts of cyberbullying can be severe, including emotional distress, depression, and even suicidal thoughts.

Global Examples and Initiatives:

- **Australia**: The Australian government has implemented the "eSafety Commissioner" initiative, which provides resources, education, and support for individuals experiencing cyberbullying. The eSafety Commissioner has the authority to investigate and remove harmful content from social media platforms.
- **United States**: Programs like "StopBullying.gov" offer tools and resources for students, parents, and educators to recognize and combat cyberbullying. The website provides guidance on how to report cyberbullying and seek support.

Privacy Concerns

Privacy concerns revolve around the unauthorized collection, use, and sharing of personal information. With the proliferation of data-driven technologies, individuals are increasingly vulnerable to privacy breaches, which can lead to identity theft, financial loss, and other harms.

Global Examples and Initiatives:

- **European Union**: The General Data Protection Regulation (GDPR) is a comprehensive legal framework designed to protect the privacy and personal data of individuals within the EU. It requires organizations to obtain explicit consent from users before collecting their data and to ensure the security of this data.

- **Brazil**: The Brazilian General Data Protection Law (LGPD) mirrors many aspects of the GDPR and aims to protect the personal data of Brazilian citizens. It imposes strict requirements on businesses regarding data collection, processing, and storage.

Data Breaches

Data breaches involve unauthorized access to confidential information, often resulting in the exposure of personal, financial, or health data. The consequences can be far-reaching, including financial loss, reputational damage, and legal ramifications.

Global Examples and Initiatives:

- **Global**: The "Cybersecurity Tech Accord" is a global initiative where more than 150 tech companies have committed to improving cybersecurity practices and protecting users from data breaches. Signatories include major companies like Microsoft, Facebook, and HP.
- **Singapore**: The Cyber Security Agency of Singapore (CSA) launched the "Go Safe Online" campaign to educate businesses and individuals about cybersecurity practices. The CSA also collaborates with international partners to enhance global cybersecurity resilience.

Initiatives Aimed at Promoting Safe and Responsible Internet Usage

Promoting safe and responsible internet usage requires collaborative efforts from governments, educational institutions, NGOs, and private organizations. Here are some notable initiatives from around the world:

Government-Led Initiatives

- **United Kingdom**: The UK government has introduced the "Online Safety Bill," which aims to regulate harmful online content and protect users, particularly children, from cyberbullying, grooming, and other online harms. The bill places a duty of care on digital platforms to ensure user safety.
- **India**: The "Digital India" initiative includes components focused on cybersecurity and safe internet practices. The program aims to enhance digital literacy across the country and includes workshops and resources on safe internet usage for students and the general public.

Educational Programs

- **Finland**: The Finnish National Agency for Education has integrated digital literacy and online safety into the national curriculum. Finnish schools teach students about responsible internet use, privacy protection, and recognizing online threats from an early age.
- **Canada**: The "MediaSmarts" program provides digital and media literacy resources to Canadian educators, parents, and youth. The program covers a wide range of topics, including online privacy, cyberbullying, and digital citizenship.

NGO and Private Sector Initiatives

- **Global**: "The Family Online Safety Institute (FOSI)" works with governments, industry, and non-profits to promote a safer online environment for families. FOSI provides resources, conducts research, and advocates for policies that support safe internet usage.
- **Africa**: The "African Cybersecurity and Digital Rights Organization (ACDRO)" aims to raise awareness about cybersecurity and digital rights across the African continent. ACDRO conducts training sessions, workshops, and advocacy campaigns to promote safe internet practices.

Community and Grassroots Efforts

- **Latin America**: The "Red PaPaz" network in Colombia engages parents, educators, and communities in promoting safe and responsible internet use among children and adolescents. Red PaPaz provides educational materials and organizes events to foster digital literacy and online safety.
- **Southeast Asia**: The "Digital Thailand Big Bang" initiative includes community outreach programs that educate citizens about cybersecurity, digital literacy, and safe internet practices. These programs are part of Thailand's broader efforts to transition to a digital economy.

Technological Solutions

- **Parental Control Software**: Tools like Qustodio, Norton Family, and Net Nanny offer parents the ability to monitor and control their children's internet usage, set time limits, and block inappropriate content.

- **Safe Browsing Tools**: Browsers like Google Chrome and Mozilla Firefox have integrated safe browsing features that warn users about potentially dangerous websites and downloads.

Conclusion

Safe internet usage is a multifaceted issue that requires a comprehensive approach involving education, regulation, and community engagement. By understanding the risks of internet addiction, cyberbullying, privacy concerns, and data breaches, and by promoting global initiatives for safe internet practices, we can create a safer digital environment for everyone.

Chapter 10:

Combating Misinformation and Fake News

Global Spread of Misinformation and Fake News

In the digital age, the rapid dissemination of information through the internet has transformed how we consume news and share information. However, this has also led to the proliferation of misinformation and fake news, posing significant challenges worldwide. Misinformation refers to false or inaccurate information spread without malicious intent, while fake news is deliberately fabricated to deceive or mislead.

The Nature of Misinformation and Fake News

The spread of misinformation and fake news is facilitated by several factors:

- **Social Media Platforms**: Platforms like Facebook, Twitter, and Instagram are powerful tools for information dissemination. Their algorithms prioritize engaging content, which can often be sensational or misleading, leading to the rapid spread of false information.
- **Echo Chambers and Filter Bubbles**: Online algorithms tend to show users content that aligns with their existing beliefs, creating echo chambers. This reinforces pre-existing biases and makes it difficult for users to encounter differing viewpoints or fact-checked information.

- **Lack of Media Literacy**: Many people lack the skills to critically evaluate online information, making them more susceptible to believing and sharing misinformation.

Global Examples of Misinformation

- **United States**: The 2016 US presidential election saw a massive surge in fake news. False stories about candidates were widely shared on social media, influencing public opinion and potentially the election outcome.
- **India**: During the COVID-19 pandemic, misinformation about cures and treatments spread widely on WhatsApp, leading to panic and dangerous behaviors.
- **Brazil**: Misinformation around the Zika virus outbreak in 2015 led to widespread fear and misinformation about the causes and prevention of the virus.

Impact of Misinformation on Societies, Democracies, and Public Health

Societal Impact

Misinformation undermines public trust in institutions, media, and experts. It can sow discord, polarize communities, and exacerbate social tensions. For instance, false information about immigration can fuel xenophobia and racism.

Impact on Democracies

Misinformation poses a severe threat to democratic processes. It can influence elections, as seen in the 2016 US presidential election and the Brexit referendum in the UK. False information about candidates, voting procedures, and policies can mislead voters and undermine the integrity of democratic institutions.

Impact on Public Health

The COVID-19 pandemic starkly illustrated the dangers of health-related misinformation. False claims about vaccines, treatments, and the virus itself spread rapidly, leading to vaccine hesitancy, disregard for public health measures, and ultimately, preventable deaths. For example, in Nigeria, misinformation about polio vaccines led to a resurgence of the disease in the early 2000s.

Strategies and Tools to Combat Misinformation

Combating misinformation requires a multifaceted approach involving technology, education, regulation, and international cooperation. Here are some effective strategies and tools being used globally:

Fact-Checking Initiatives

Fact-checking organizations play a crucial role in verifying information and debunking false claims. These organizations use rigorous methodologies to assess the accuracy of information and provide corrections. Examples include:

- **Africa Check (Africa)**: Africa Check verifies claims made by public figures, institutions, and the media across the continent.
- **Politifact (United States)**: Politifact rates the accuracy of claims made by politicians and public figures in the US.
- **Alt News (India)**: Alt News focuses on debunking false information circulating on social media and mainstream media in India.

Digital Literacy Programs

Improving digital literacy is essential for empowering individuals to critically evaluate online information and recognize misinformation. Educational programs and campaigns can help people develop these skills:

- **MediaSmarts (Canada)**: MediaSmarts provides resources for educators, parents, and youth to develop critical thinking skills and navigate the digital media landscape responsibly.
- **eSafety Commissioner (Australia)**: This initiative offers educational resources and workshops to help Australians recognize and respond to online misinformation.
- **Digital Literacy Training (Singapore)**: The Infocomm Media Development Authority (IMDA) in Singapore runs digital literacy programs aimed at helping citizens critically assess online information.

Technological Solutions

Technology companies and researchers are developing tools to detect and limit the spread of misinformation:

- **Algorithm Adjustments**: Social media platforms like Facebook and Twitter have adjusted their algorithms to reduce the visibility of false information and prioritize reliable sources.
- **AI and Machine Learning**: Tools like Google's Fact Check Explorer use AI to identify and highlight fact-checked content in search results.
- **Browser Extensions**: Extensions like NewsGuard and Factual can be installed on browsers to provide credibility ratings for news websites and alert users to potentially false information.

Government and Policy Interventions

Governments can play a crucial role in combating misinformation through regulation and policy measures:

- **EU Code of Practice on Disinformation (European Union)**: The EU has established a voluntary code for tech companies to follow in order to reduce the spread of misinformation.
- **Communications and Multimedia Act (Malaysia)**: This law includes provisions against spreading false information and allows for legal action against those who do so.

Community and Grassroots Efforts

Community-based initiatives can effectively combat misinformation by leveraging local knowledge and networks:

- **Red PaPaz (Colombia)**: This network of parents and educators in Colombia works to combat misinformation by providing accurate information and educational resources on health and safety.
- **AfricaCheck's Community Outreach (Africa)**: Africa Check engages with communities through workshops and events to raise awareness about misinformation and promote fact-checking practices.

Popular Examples of Misinformation Cases

- **COVID-19 Pandemic**: False claims about the origins, prevention, and treatment of COVID-19 spread rapidly. Examples include misinformation about 5G technology causing the virus and the promotion of unproven treatments like hydroxychloroquine.
- **Election Misinformation**: In the 2020 US presidential election, false claims about mail-in voting fraud were widely circulated, leading to confusion and mistrust in the electoral process.
- **Climate Change Denial**: Misinformation about climate change, often spread by interest groups, has impeded global efforts to address environmental issues.

Tools and Platforms for Fact-Checking and Combating Misinformation

- **Snopes**: One of the oldest fact-checking websites, Snopes debunks a wide range of misinformation, from urban legends to political claims.
- **FactCheck.org**: This project of the Annenberg Public Policy Center provides thorough analyses of political statements and claims.
- **First Draft**: This organization provides tools and resources for journalists to identify and report on misinformation.

Conclusion

Combating misinformation and fake news is a global challenge that requires concerted efforts across multiple sectors. By understanding the nature and impact of misinformation, employing effective strategies and tools, and fostering a culture of critical thinking and digital literacy, we can mitigate the harmful effects of false information and build a more informed and resilient society.

Chapter 11:

Digital Literacy and Inclusivity

Digital Literacy Disparities Among Different Demographics

Gender Disparities

Digital literacy gaps between genders are significant in many parts of the world. Women and girls often have less access to digital technologies and training compared to men and boys. This disparity is driven by various factors including cultural norms, economic barriers, and educational inequalities.

Global Examples:

- **Sub-Saharan Africa:** In many countries in this region, women are 50% less likely to use the internet than men. Cultural norms that prioritize male education and economic participation often restrict women's access to digital tools and literacy programs.
- **South Asia:** In countries like India and Pakistan, women face social and cultural barriers that limit their access to digital devices and the internet. Initiatives like the "Internet Saathi" program by Google and Tata Trusts have aimed to bridge this gap by training rural women to use smartphones and the internet, empowering them to teach others in their communities.

Age Disparities

The digital literacy gap also exists across different age groups. Younger generations, often referred to as digital natives, generally have higher levels of digital literacy due to growing up with technology. In contrast, older adults, or digital immigrants, may struggle with adopting new technologies.

Global Examples:

- **Europe:** Countries like Germany and Sweden have implemented programs to help older adults gain digital skills. The "Silver Surfers" initiative in the UK offers training sessions for seniors to learn how to use the internet and digital devices.
- **Japan:** With one of the oldest populations in the world, Japan has launched the "Digital Supporters" program where volunteers teach elderly citizens how to navigate digital technologies, helping them stay connected and independent.

Socioeconomic Disparities

Socioeconomic status significantly impacts digital literacy. Individuals from low-income backgrounds often have less access to digital devices and the internet, which hinders their ability to develop digital skills.

Global Examples:

- **United States:** In economically disadvantaged areas, programs like "EveryoneOn" work to provide affordable internet access and digital literacy training to low-income families.

- **Brazil:** The "Computers for Schools" program donates refurbished computers to schools in low-income areas, coupled with training for students and teachers, to promote digital literacy and bridge the socioeconomic gap.

Initiatives and Programs Aimed at Bridging the Digital Divide

Government Initiatives

Governments worldwide recognize the importance of digital literacy and have implemented various initiatives to address disparities.

Global Examples:

- **Australia:** The "Be Connected" initiative by the Australian government offers free courses and resources to help older Australians gain digital skills and confidence online.
- **Kenya:** The Kenyan government has launched the "Digital Literacy Programme," which aims to provide digital devices and training to primary school students and teachers across the country, ensuring early exposure to digital skills.

Non-Governmental Organizations (NGOs)

NGOs play a crucial role in promoting digital literacy and inclusivity, often targeting marginalized communities.

Global Examples:

- **South Africa:** The "Zenzeleni Networks" project in rural Eastern Cape provides community-owned internet infrastructure, along with training programs to enhance digital skills and economic opportunities for local residents.
- **Bangladesh:** BRAC, one of the largest NGOs in the world, runs digital literacy programs for women and young people in rural areas, focusing on building skills for education and employment.

Corporate Social Responsibility (CSR) Programs

Many corporations have launched CSR initiatives to support digital literacy and inclusivity.

Global Examples:

- **Microsoft's "Digital Skills for Africa"**: This program offers free online courses, certifications, and resources to help young Africans develop skills needed for the digital economy.
- **Huawei's "Seeds for the Future"**: This global program provides training and development opportunities for young people in ICT, aiming to foster talent and bridge the digital divide.

Success Stories of Marginalized Communities Gaining Empowerment Through Digital Literacy

Empowerment Through Education

Access to digital literacy can transform educational opportunities for marginalized communities.

Global Examples:

- **Rwanda:** The "One Laptop per Child" initiative has distributed laptops to primary school children across Rwanda, significantly improving digital literacy and educational outcomes in rural areas.
- **Peru:** The "Huascarán Project" by the Ministry of Education aims to integrate ICT into the education system, particularly in remote and rural areas, enhancing both teacher and student digital competencies.

Economic Empowerment

Digital literacy empowers individuals to participate in the digital economy, leading to improved economic opportunities.

Global Examples:

- **India:** The "Digital India" campaign aims to transform India into a digitally empowered society. Programs like "Pradhan Mantri Gramin Digital Saksharta Abhiyan" (PMGDISHA) focus on providing digital literacy to rural households, enabling them to access online services and improve their livelihoods.

- **Nigeria:** The "Digital Girls Club" initiative by Tech4Dev equips young women with digital skills, enhancing their employability and entrepreneurial potential in the tech industry.

Social and Civic Empowerment

Digital literacy fosters greater social and civic participation, allowing marginalized communities to engage more fully in society.

Global Examples:

- **Indonesia:** The "Desa Digital" (Digital Village) program aims to bring digital services to rural communities, enhancing access to information, government services, and opportunities for civic engagement.
- **Mexico:** The "Rural Digital Inclusion" project by Fundación Carlos Slim provides training and internet access to rural communities, empowering them to participate in social, educational, and economic activities online.

Bridging Cultural and Language Barriers

Digital literacy programs often include efforts to make digital tools and content accessible in local languages and culturally relevant formats.

Global Examples:

- **Papua New Guinea:** The "Library For All" project creates digital libraries with content tailored to local languages and cultural contexts, promoting literacy and digital skills in remote communities.

- **Morocco:** The "Tifinagh Keyboard" initiative provides Amazigh-speaking communities with digital tools in their native script, facilitating greater access to technology and online resources.

Conclusion

Digital literacy and inclusivity are critical components of a just and equitable digital society. By addressing disparities among different demographics and implementing targeted initiatives, we can empower marginalized communities, enhance their participation in the digital world, and create opportunities for social and economic development globally. Through government programs, NGO efforts, and corporate initiatives, the digital divide can be bridged, fostering a more inclusive and digitally literate world for all.

Chapter 12:

Global Case Studies in Digital Literacy

Detailed Case Studies of Countries and Regions That Have Made Significant Strides in Digital Literacy

Finland: A Model for Digital Literacy Education

Overview Finland consistently ranks at the top of global education systems, and its approach to digital literacy is no exception. The Finnish education system integrates digital literacy from an early age, ensuring that students develop critical digital skills as part of their overall education.

Key Initiatives

- **Curriculum Integration**: Digital literacy is embedded across all subjects rather than being taught as a standalone subject. This holistic approach ensures that students see digital skills as integral to all areas of learning and life.
- **Teacher Training**: Continuous professional development for teachers includes training on integrating digital tools and teaching digital literacy, ensuring educators are well-equipped to guide students.
- **Public Libraries and Community Centers**: These institutions offer free access to digital tools and training for people of all ages, promoting lifelong learning and digital inclusion.

Outcomes: Finland's integrated approach has resulted in a highly digitally literate population. Students are not only proficient in using digital tools but also critical thinkers who can navigate the digital landscape effectively.

Singapore: Smart Nation Initiative

Overview: Singapore's Smart Nation initiative aims to transform the country through technology, creating a digitally savvy population and leveraging technology to improve everyday life.

Key Initiatives

- **Digital Readiness Blueprint**: This framework outlines strategies to ensure all Singaporeans can participate in the digital economy. It includes initiatives like subsidized internet access for low-income families and digital literacy programs for seniors.
- **SkillsFuture**: A national movement that provides Singaporeans with opportunities to develop skills relevant to the digital economy through courses, workshops, and on-the-job training.
- **Public-Private Partnerships**: Collaboration between the government and tech companies to provide resources, training, and support for digital literacy initiatives.

Outcomes: Singapore has achieved high levels of digital literacy across its population. The Smart Nation initiative has not only enhanced digital skills but also fostered innovation and economic growth.

Estonia: E-Government and Digital Citizenship

Overview: Estonia is renowned for its advanced e-government services and commitment to digital citizenship. The country has transformed itself into one of the most digitally advanced nations in the world.

Key Initiatives

- **E-Residency Program**: This initiative allows non-Estonians to start and manage a business online, promoting global entrepreneurship and digital literacy.
- **Digital ID System**: Every Estonian citizen has a digital ID, which they use to access a wide range of e-services, from voting to healthcare.
- **Digital Education Programs**: Schools and universities in Estonia incorporate digital literacy into their curricula, ensuring students are well-prepared for the digital world.

Outcomes: Estonia's focus on digital literacy and e-governance has resulted in a highly connected society. Citizens are adept at using digital tools for everyday tasks, and the country's digital economy is thriving.

Rwanda: Transforming Through Technology

Overview: Rwanda has made significant strides in digital literacy and technology integration, transforming itself into a regional ICT hub despite its history of conflict.

Key Initiatives

- **One Laptop Per Child (OLPC)**: This program provides laptops to primary school children, ensuring early exposure to digital tools and skills.
- **Digital Ambassadors Program**: This initiative trains young people to become digital ambassadors who then teach digital skills in their communities.
- **ICT Hubs and Innovation Centers**: Kigali, the capital city, hosts several tech hubs and innovation centers that provide training, resources, and support for digital entrepreneurs.

Outcomes: Rwanda's commitment to digital literacy has fostered a new generation of tech-savvy citizens. The country's focus on ICT has also attracted foreign investment and boosted economic development.

Brazil: Bridging the Digital Divide

Overview: Brazil faces significant challenges in terms of digital literacy, particularly in its vast and diverse regions. However, targeted programs have made notable progress in bridging the digital divide.

Key Initiatives

- **Computers for Schools Program**: This government initiative donates refurbished computers to schools in low-income areas and provides training for students and teachers.
- **LAN Houses (Internet Cafés)**: These community-run internet cafés provide affordable access to the internet and digital literacy training in underserved areas.
- **Telecentros (Telecenters)**: Public access points that offer free internet access and digital literacy courses, particularly in rural and marginalized communities.

Outcomes: Brazil's initiatives have improved digital literacy rates, particularly among young people and in rural areas. The country continues to work towards greater digital inclusion and literacy.

Lessons Learned from Successful Digital Literacy Programs and Policies

Integration and Holistic Approaches

Countries like Finland and Singapore show that integrating digital literacy across curricula and societal structures is highly effective. Embedding digital skills into all aspects of education and daily life ensures comprehensive and practical digital literacy development.

Importance of Teacher Training

Equipping educators with the skills and knowledge to teach digital literacy is crucial. Continuous professional development, as seen in Finland, ensures that teachers can effectively integrate digital tools into their teaching.

Public-Private Partnerships

Collaboration between governments and private sector organizations can enhance the reach and impact of digital literacy initiatives. Singapore's Smart Nation initiative and Rwanda's tech hubs exemplify successful public-private partnerships.

Community Engagement and Empowerment

Engaging communities and leveraging local knowledge and resources can significantly enhance digital literacy efforts. Rwanda's Digital Ambassadors Program and Brazil's LAN Houses demonstrate the power of community-driven initiatives.

Accessibility and Inclusivity

Ensuring that digital literacy programs are accessible to all, particularly marginalized and underserved communities, is essential. Programs like Singapore's Digital Readiness Blueprint and Estonia's e-Residency highlight the importance of inclusivity in digital literacy efforts.

Comparative Analysis of Different Approaches to Improving Digital Literacy

Government-Led Initiatives

Government-led initiatives, such as those in Finland and Singapore, are often comprehensive and well-funded, allowing for wide-scale impact. These programs typically involve policy frameworks, public funding, and national strategies to ensure digital literacy for all citizens.

NGO and Community-Based Programs

NGO and community-based programs, like those in South Africa and Bangladesh, are crucial for reaching marginalized populations and addressing specific local needs. These programs often rely on grassroots efforts and community engagement to drive digital literacy.

Corporate Social Responsibility (CSR) Efforts

Corporate initiatives, such as Microsoft's Digital Skills for Africa, play a significant role in promoting digital literacy through funding, resources, and training. These programs often complement government and NGO efforts, providing additional support and expertise.

Hybrid Approaches

Combining elements from government, NGO, and corporate efforts can create a powerful synergy. Rwanda's approach, which involves government programs, community engagement, and private sector support, exemplifies the effectiveness of hybrid strategies in improving digital literacy.

Conclusion

Digital literacy is a critical component of modern society, enabling individuals to participate fully in the digital economy and access essential services. By examining global case studies, we can learn valuable lessons and identify effective strategies for promoting digital literacy and inclusivity worldwide. Through comprehensive and inclusive approaches, we can bridge the digital divide and empower all individuals to thrive in the digital age.

Chapter 13:

The Role of Artificial Intelligence in Digital Literacy

Examination of How AI Technologies Are Being Used to Enhance Digital Literacy

Artificial Intelligence (AI) has emerged as a transformative force in various sectors, and education is no exception. AI technologies are being harnessed to enhance digital literacy, providing innovative solutions that cater to diverse learning needs. These technologies are making education more accessible, personalized, and efficient.

Personalized Learning

One of the most significant contributions of AI in digital literacy is personalized learning. AI algorithms analyze students' learning patterns and preferences, enabling the creation of customized educational experiences. This approach ensures that each learner receives content tailored to their specific needs, thereby improving engagement and retention.

Examples:

- **China**: Platforms like Squirrel AI use adaptive learning systems to offer personalized education experiences to millions of students. The AI-driven platform adjusts the difficulty level and content based on individual student performance.

- **USA**: DreamBox Learning provides a mathematics education platform that adapts to the user's proficiency level, offering a tailored learning path for each student.

Intelligent Tutoring Systems

AI-driven intelligent tutoring systems (ITS) simulate one-on-one tutoring by providing personalized feedback and guidance. These systems help students understand complex concepts and improve their problem-solving skills.

Examples:

- **India**: BYJU'S, an edtech company, uses AI to provide interactive learning experiences through video lessons and personalized tutoring. The platform's AI algorithms adjust the learning path based on the student's performance and progress.
- **Europe**: CENTURY Tech, a UK-based company, employs AI to create personalized learning plans that adapt in real-time to students' needs, enhancing their understanding and retention of knowledge.

Natural Language Processing (NLP)

NLP enables AI systems to understand and interact with human language, facilitating more intuitive and effective learning experiences. AI-powered chatbots and virtual assistants leverage NLP to provide instant support and feedback to students.

Examples:

- **Australia**: The University of New South Wales uses AI-powered chatbots to assist students with administrative tasks and academic queries, improving their overall educational experience.
- **South Africa**: Siyavula, an edtech company, employs AI-driven chatbots to provide students with instant feedback on their assignments, helping them understand their mistakes and learn more effectively.

Gamification and Interactive Learning

AI enhances gamification and interactive learning by creating dynamic and engaging educational content. AI-driven platforms use game-like elements to make learning more enjoyable and effective.

Examples:

- **South America**: In Brazil, Geekie Labs uses AI to offer gamified learning experiences that adapt to each student's level, making education more engaging and effective.
- **Japan**: Arcterus Inc.'s platform, STUDYing, uses AI to gamify the learning process, providing students with interactive and engaging content that adapts to their learning pace.

Case Studies of AI-Driven Educational Tools and Platforms

Coursera and EdX: Global Reach and Personalization

Overview: Coursera and EdX are among the most popular online learning platforms, offering a wide range of courses from top universities and institutions worldwide. Both platforms leverage AI to enhance the learning experience.

AI Features

- **Personalized Recommendations**: AI algorithms suggest courses and content based on the learner's interests, previous courses, and performance.
- **Automated Grading**: AI systems grade assignments and quizzes, providing instant feedback and freeing up time for instructors to focus on more complex tasks.
- **Interactive Content**: AI enhances interactive content, such as simulations and virtual labs, making learning more immersive and effective.

Global Impact: Coursera and EdX have democratized access to quality education, reaching millions of learners across the globe. By leveraging AI, these platforms have made learning more personalized and accessible, catering to diverse educational needs.

Duolingo: Language Learning Through AI

Overview: Duolingo is a popular language-learning app that uses AI to offer personalized and engaging language education to users worldwide.

AI Features

- **Adaptive Learning**: Duolingo's AI algorithms adjust the difficulty level of lessons based on the user's proficiency and progress.
- **Instant Feedback**: The app provides instant feedback on exercises, helping users learn from their mistakes in real-time.
- **Gamification**: Duolingo uses gamified elements, such as points, levels, and rewards, to make language learning fun and motivating.

Global Impact: Duolingo has made language learning accessible to millions of people, regardless of their location or background. The app's AI-driven approach has revolutionized language education, making it more personalized and effective.

Alibaba's AI Classrooms: Transforming Education in China

Overview: Alibaba, the Chinese e-commerce giant, has ventured into education with its AI-powered classrooms, aiming to improve education quality in rural and underserved areas of China.

AI Features

- **Facial Recognition**: AI systems use facial recognition to monitor student engagement and attention, providing real-time feedback to teachers.
- **Personalized Learning Plans**: AI creates personalized learning plans for students based on their performance and learning needs.

- **Interactive Content**: The platform offers interactive and engaging educational content, making learning more effective and enjoyable.

Impact: Alibaba's AI classrooms have improved education quality in remote and rural areas of China, bridging the gap between urban and rural education. The AI-driven approach ensures that all students receive a quality education, regardless of their location.

NetDragon: AI in Education Across Africa

Overview: NetDragon, a Chinese technology company, is using AI to enhance education across Africa, providing digital learning solutions to schools and institutions.

AI Features

- **Adaptive Learning**: The platform offers adaptive learning solutions that adjust to the student's level and pace.
- **Virtual Classrooms**: AI-powered virtual classrooms provide interactive and engaging learning experiences.
- **Teacher Training**: AI-driven training programs help teachers integrate digital tools into their teaching, improving overall education quality.

Impact: NetDragon's AI-driven education solutions have improved access to quality education in various African countries, empowering students and teachers with the tools they need to succeed in the digital age.

Ethical Implications of Using AI in Digital Education

Data Privacy and Security

AI systems rely on vast amounts of data to function effectively. This raises concerns about data privacy and security, as sensitive information about students' learning habits and personal details is collected and analyzed.

Concerns

- **Data Breaches**: Unauthorized access to student data can lead to privacy breaches and misuse of information.
- **Informed Consent**: Students and parents need to be fully informed about how their data is being used and should have the option to opt-out if they are uncomfortable.

Mitigation Strategies

- **Robust Security Measures**: Implementing strong data encryption and security protocols to protect student data.
- **Transparency and Consent**: Clearly communicating data usage policies and obtaining informed consent from users.

Bias and Fairness

AI systems can inadvertently perpetuate biases present in the data they are trained on, leading to unfair and biased outcomes in education.

Concerns

- **Algorithmic Bias**: AI algorithms may favor certain groups over others, leading to unequal educational opportunities.
- **Lack of Diversity in Data**: Using homogeneous data sets can result in AI systems that do not cater to diverse learning needs.

Mitigation Strategies

- **Diverse Data Sets**: Ensuring that AI systems are trained on diverse data sets to minimize bias.
- **Regular Audits**: Conducting regular audits of AI systems to identify and address any biases.

Human-AI Interaction

The increasing reliance on AI in education raises questions about the role of human teachers and the quality of human-AI interaction.

Concerns

- **Depersonalization**: Over-reliance on AI could lead to a lack of personal interaction between teachers and students.
- **Job Displacement**: AI systems could potentially replace certain teaching roles, leading to job displacement.

Mitigation Strategies

- **Augmenting, Not Replacing**: Using AI to augment human teaching, providing support and resources rather than replacing teachers.
- **Human Oversight**: Ensuring that human educators are involved in the development and deployment of AI systems to maintain the human touch in education.

Conclusion

AI has the potential to revolutionize digital literacy by providing personalized, engaging, and efficient learning experiences. However, it is crucial to address the ethical implications associated with AI in education to ensure that these technologies are used responsibly and equitably. By examining global case studies and considering the ethical challenges, we can harness the power of AI to enhance digital literacy and create a more inclusive and effective education system.

Chapter 14:

Digital Literacy in Healthcare

Impact of Digital Literacy on Healthcare Access and Quality

Digital literacy plays a crucial role in transforming healthcare access and quality. As healthcare systems around the world embrace digital technologies, the ability of individuals to effectively use these tools becomes paramount. Digital literacy empowers patients to access information, engage with healthcare providers, and manage their health more effectively.

Improved Access to Healthcare Services

Digital literacy enables patients to navigate online healthcare platforms, book appointments, and consult with doctors through telemedicine. This is especially beneficial in remote or underserved areas where healthcare services are scarce.

Examples:

- **India**: Telemedicine platforms like Practo and 1mg have revolutionized access to healthcare by providing online consultations, diagnostics, and medication delivery. These platforms have significantly improved access to healthcare in rural areas.
- **Canada**: The Maple platform allows Canadians to connect with healthcare professionals online, providing access to medical advice and prescriptions without the

need for in-person visits, particularly useful in remote regions.

Enhanced Patient Engagement and Self-Management

Digital literacy helps patients understand and utilize health information, leading to better self-management of chronic conditions and overall health. Access to online health records and patient portals allows individuals to track their health metrics, view test results, and communicate with healthcare providers.

Examples:

- **United States**: The MyChart app, used by many healthcare systems, allows patients to access their medical records, communicate with doctors, and manage appointments. This has increased patient engagement and satisfaction.
- **Australia**: The My Health Record system provides Australians with a digital summary of their health information, promoting self-management and continuity of care.

Improved Quality of Care

Digital literacy enables healthcare providers to use electronic health records (EHRs), telemedicine, and other digital tools effectively, leading to better coordination of care and improved patient outcomes. Digital tools also facilitate the collection and analysis of health data, enabling evidence-based decision-making.

Examples:

- **United Kingdom**: The National Health Service (NHS) has implemented EHR systems across hospitals and clinics, improving the quality and efficiency of care through better data management and coordination.
- **Kenya**: The AMPATH program uses digital tools to manage patient records and deliver HIV care, resulting in improved patient outcomes and streamlined care delivery.

How Digital Tools Are Transforming Patient Care, Medical Research, and Public Health

Digital tools are revolutionizing patient care, medical research, and public health by enabling more efficient, accurate, and accessible healthcare solutions.

Patient Care

Digital tools such as telemedicine, mobile health apps, and wearable devices are transforming patient care by providing real-time monitoring, personalized treatment plans, and remote consultations.

Telemedicine: Telemedicine allows patients to consult with healthcare providers remotely, reducing the need for in-person visits and expanding access to care.

Examples:

- **Brazil**: The Teleradiology Solutions platform provides remote radiology services, enabling timely diagnosis and treatment for patients in underserved areas.

- **China**: Ping An Good Doctor offers telemedicine services, allowing millions of Chinese patients to access healthcare advice and consultations online.

Mobile Health Apps and Wearables: Mobile health apps and wearable devices help patients monitor their health in real-time, providing valuable data to both patients and healthcare providers.

Examples:

- **Germany**: Ada Health's app uses AI to provide users with personalized health assessments, guiding them to appropriate care based on their symptoms.
- **South Africa**: The Vula app connects healthcare workers in rural areas with specialists, improving patient care and outcomes.

Medical Research

Digital tools are accelerating medical research by enabling the collection, analysis, and sharing of vast amounts of health data. This leads to faster discoveries, more effective treatments, and personalized medicine.

Examples:

- **United States**: The All of Us Research Program aims to gather health data from diverse populations to advance precision medicine. Digital tools facilitate data collection and participant engagement.
- **Japan**: The Tohoku Medical Megabank Project uses digital health records and biobanking to conduct

longitudinal health studies, contributing to medical research and public health.

Public Health

Digital tools are enhancing public health by improving disease surveillance, outbreak response, and health education. They enable the collection and analysis of health data, informing public health strategies and interventions.

Examples:

- **Nigeria**: The eHealth Africa platform uses digital tools to improve disease surveillance and response, particularly for infectious diseases like Ebola and COVID-19.
- **Thailand**: The Smart Health program integrates digital health records and telemedicine to enhance public health services and disease management.

Challenges and Opportunities in Educating the Public About Digital Health Resources

Educating the public about digital health resources presents both challenges and opportunities. Addressing these challenges is crucial to ensure that everyone can benefit from digital healthcare solutions.

Challenges

1. **Digital Divide**

   - **Issue**: Limited access to digital devices and the internet can prevent individuals from utilizing digital health resources.
   - **Example**: In rural areas of sub-Saharan Africa, lack of internet connectivity and smartphones hinders access to telemedicine and digital health information.

2. **Low Digital Literacy**

- **Issue**: A lack of digital literacy skills can prevent individuals from effectively using digital health tools.
- **Example**: Older adults in many countries, including the United States and Japan, often struggle with using digital health platforms due to limited digital literacy.

3. **Privacy and Security Concerns**

- **Issue**: Concerns about data privacy and security can deter people from using digital health resources.
- **Example**: In Europe, strict GDPR regulations aim to protect personal data, but also pose challenges for the implementation of digital health solutions.

Opportunities

1. **Digital Health Education Programs**

- **Opportunity**: Implementing education programs to improve digital literacy and familiarize individuals with digital health tools.
- **Example**: In Australia, the government has launched the Be Connected program to help older adults improve their digital skills, including the use of digital health resources.

2. **Community-Based Initiatives**

- **Opportunity**: Leveraging community centers, libraries, and local organizations to provide digital health education and support.
- **Example**: In India, the Digital Empowerment Foundation runs programs in rural areas to teach digital literacy and promote the use of digital health tools.

3. **Public-Private Partnerships**

- **Opportunity**: Collaborating between governments, private companies, and NGOs to develop and disseminate digital health resources.
- **Example**: In Kenya, the M-TIBA platform, a collaboration between the government, Safaricom, and PharmAccess, provides mobile health wallets to improve access to healthcare services.

4. **Mobile and User-Friendly Solutions**

- **Opportunity**: Developing mobile-friendly and easy-to-use digital health tools to ensure broader accessibility.
- **Example**: In Bangladesh, the Aponjon service provides maternal and child health information via SMS, making it accessible to women with basic mobile phones.

Success Stories

1. **Rwanda**

- **Initiative**: The government of Rwanda, in partnership with Babyl, a digital health provider, has implemented a nationwide telemedicine service.
- **Impact**: This initiative has improved access to healthcare for millions of Rwandans, particularly in rural areas.

2. **Canada**

- **Initiative**: The Digital Health Canada organization provides resources and training to healthcare professionals and the public on digital health tools and technologies.
- **Impact**: These efforts have increased the adoption and effective use of digital health resources across the country.

3. **Chile**

- **Initiative**: The Fundación País Digital runs programs to improve digital literacy and promote the use of digital health tools among Chilean citizens.

- **Impact**: These programs have enhanced digital literacy and healthcare access, particularly in underserved communities.

Conclusion

Digital literacy is a vital component of modern healthcare. It enhances access to services, improves patient care, and accelerates medical research. Despite the challenges, numerous opportunities exist to educate the public about digital health resources and ensure that everyone can benefit from the advancements in digital healthcare. By examining global examples and addressing the challenges, we can foster a more digitally literate and healthier world.

Chapter 15:

The Future of Digital Literacy in the 4IR

Predictions and Scenarios for the Future Development of Digital Literacy

As we progress further into the Fourth Industrial Revolution (4IR), digital literacy will continue to evolve, driven by rapid technological advancements. The future development of digital literacy can be envisaged through various predictions and scenarios that highlight its critical role in our interconnected world.

Increased Integration of AI and Automation

Artificial intelligence (AI) and automation will increasingly permeate various aspects of daily life and work. Digital literacy will expand to include a comprehensive understanding of AI tools, machine learning, and automation technologies.

Examples:

- **United States**: AI-driven personal assistants like Amazon's Alexa and Apple's Siri are becoming more sophisticated, requiring users to understand how to interact with these systems effectively.
- **China**: The widespread use of AI in smart city initiatives, such as in Shenzhen, necessitates a populace that can navigate and utilize AI-driven public services.

Emergence of New Digital Platforms and Tools

The continuous development of new digital platforms and tools will demand that individuals constantly update their digital literacy skills. This includes new social media platforms, collaborative tools, and virtual reality environments.

Examples:

- **South Korea**: The rise of virtual influencers on platforms like Instagram and TikTok requires users to discern digital personas and the implications of interacting with AI-generated content.
- **Nigeria**: The adoption of mobile banking and fintech solutions like Paga necessitates a robust understanding of digital financial tools.

Expansion of Digital Learning and Education

The future will see a significant shift towards digital learning environments. Educational institutions will increasingly rely on digital platforms to deliver content, requiring both educators and students to be proficient in digital literacy.

Examples:

- **India**: Initiatives like the Digital India campaign are fostering digital literacy through online education platforms, ensuring that students in remote areas have access to quality education.
- **Australia**: The widespread use of learning management systems (LMS) in universities demands that students and faculty alike are adept at navigating digital learning environments.

- ## **Potential Advancements in Technology and Their Implications for Digital Literacy**

The next wave of technological advancements will significantly impact digital literacy. Understanding these technologies and their implications will be crucial for individuals to thrive in the 4IR.

Quantum Computing

Quantum computing promises to revolutionize fields such as cryptography, material science, and complex system simulations. Digital literacy will need to encompass an understanding of quantum principles and their applications.

Implications:

- Enhanced data security through quantum encryption.
- Advanced problem-solving capabilities in various scientific fields.

Blockchain and Decentralized Technologies

Blockchain technology and decentralized networks will continue to grow, influencing areas such as finance, supply chain management, and digital identity verification.

Implications:

- Improved transparency and security in transactions.
- Increased need for understanding blockchain concepts and applications.

Examples:

- **Brazil**: The use of blockchain for land registry and electoral processes ensures transparency and reduces fraud.
- **Estonia**: A pioneer in digital identity, Estonia's e-Residency program leverages blockchain to provide secure digital services.

Augmented Reality (AR) and Virtual Reality (VR)

AR and VR technologies will become more prevalent in education, entertainment, and professional training. Digital literacy will include the ability to navigate and create content within these immersive environments.

Implications:

- Enhanced learning experiences through immersive educational tools.
- New forms of entertainment and social interaction.

Examples:

- **Japan**: The use of VR in medical training enhances the practical skills of healthcare professionals.
- **Kenya**: AR applications in agriculture provide farmers with real-time information on crop health and weather conditions.

Philosophical and Ethical Considerations About the Future of Human Interaction with Digital Technologies

As digital technologies become more integrated into our lives, it is crucial to consider the philosophical and ethical implications of this integration. These considerations will shape the development and application of digital literacy in the future.

Digital Equity and Inclusion

Ensuring equitable access to digital technologies and education is essential to prevent further widening of the digital divide. Efforts must be made to provide digital literacy resources to underserved populations.

Examples:

- **South Africa**: The government's initiatives to provide free Wi-Fi in public spaces aim to bridge the digital divide and promote digital literacy.
- **Rural India**: NGOs like Pratham are working to enhance digital literacy among rural children, providing them with the skills needed to succeed in a digital world.

Data Privacy and Security

As individuals share more personal information online, concerns about data privacy and security become paramount. Digital literacy must include understanding how to protect one's digital footprint and personal data.

Examples:

- **European Union**: The General Data Protection Regulation (GDPR) sets a high standard for data protection, emphasizing the importance of digital literacy in understanding privacy rights.
- **Canada**: The Office of the Privacy Commissioner provides resources and guidelines to help citizens protect their personal information online.

Ethical Use of AI and Automation

The ethical implications of AI and automation, including issues of bias, accountability, and transparency, must be addressed. Digital literacy programs should teach individuals how to critically evaluate AI systems and their impact on society.

Examples:

- **United States**: The AI Now Institute advocates for ethical AI practices and provides resources to understand the social implications of AI technologies.
- **Germany**: The Ethics Commission on Automated and Connected Driving outlines principles for the ethical use of autonomous vehicles.

Human-Centric Design and Technology

Future technologies should prioritize human well-being and be designed with user experience in mind. Digital literacy should encompass an understanding of human-centric design principles.

Examples:

- **Scandinavia**: Countries like Sweden and Denmark emphasize human-centric design in their smart city initiatives, ensuring that technology serves the needs of the people.
- **New Zealand**: The Digital Inclusion Blueprint aims to create a user-friendly digital environment that enhances the well-being of all citizens.

Conclusion

The future of digital literacy in the 4IR will be shaped by rapid technological advancements, increased integration of digital tools, and a focus on ethical and philosophical considerations. By preparing for these changes and ensuring that digital literacy encompasses a broad range of skills and knowledge, we can create a more inclusive, equitable, and empowered global society.

Chapter 16:

Digital Literacy in Developing Countries

Challenges and Opportunities Specific to Developing Countries in Enhancing Digital Literacy

Enhancing digital literacy in developing countries presents unique challenges and opportunities. These regions often face significant barriers, such as limited access to technology, insufficient infrastructure, and socio-economic disparities. However, these challenges also create opportunities for innovative solutions and impactful interventions.

Challenges

1. **Limited Access to Technology**

- **Infrastructure Gaps**: Many developing countries lack the necessary infrastructure, such as reliable electricity and internet connectivity, to support widespread digital literacy.

Example: In rural areas of Sub-Saharan Africa, only about 22% of the population has access to electricity, making it difficult to power digital devices.

- **Cost Barriers**: The high cost of digital devices and internet access is prohibitive for many people.

Example: In South Asia, a smartphone can cost more than a month's salary for a low-income worker.

2. **Educational Disparities**

- **Lack of Trained Educators**: There is often a shortage of teachers who are proficient in digital skills and can effectively integrate technology into the curriculum.

Example: In many parts of Latin America, teachers receive minimal training in digital literacy, limiting their ability to teach these skills to students.

- **Inadequate Curriculum**: Existing educational curriculums may not prioritize or include digital literacy.

Example: In several Southeast Asian countries, digital literacy is not yet a mandatory part of the school curriculum.

3. **Socio-Economic and Cultural Barriers**

- **Gender Disparities**: Cultural norms and socio-economic factors often result in lower digital literacy rates among women and girls.

Example: In parts of the Middle East and North Africa, women are 50% less likely to use the internet compared to men.

- **Language Barriers**: A lack of digital content in local languages can hinder learning.

Example: Many digital resources are only available in English, which is not widely spoken in many regions of Africa and Asia.

Opportunities

1. **Mobile Technology**

- **High Mobile Penetration**: Mobile phones are more accessible than other digital devices, providing a platform for digital literacy.

Example: In Kenya, mobile phone penetration is over 80%, enabling the use of mobile-based educational programs like Eneza Education.

2. **Community-Based Initiatives**

- **Local Engagement**: Leveraging community centers and local organizations can facilitate digital literacy programs tailored to specific community needs.

Example: The Digital Ambassadors Program in Rwanda trains local youth to educate their communities about digital literacy.

3. **Public-Private Partnerships**

- **Collaborative Efforts**: Partnerships between governments, NGOs, and private companies can create comprehensive digital literacy initiatives.

Example: India's Digital India program involves collaboration between the government and tech companies to improve digital infrastructure and literacy.

Successful Initiatives and Programs in Developing Regions

Several successful initiatives and programs have emerged in developing regions, demonstrating effective strategies to enhance digital literacy. These programs often combine local insights with innovative approaches to overcome the unique challenges faced by these regions.

Africa

Kenya - Digital Literacy Programme (DLP)

- **Overview**: Launched by the Kenyan government, the DLP aims to integrate ICT into primary education by providing digital devices to schools and training teachers.
- **Impact**: Over 1 million devices have been distributed, and thousands of teachers have been trained, significantly increasing digital literacy among young students.

Rwanda - Digital Ambassadors Program

- **Overview**: This program trains young people to become digital ambassadors who then teach digital literacy skills in their communities.
- **Impact**: The program has reached over 5,000 people, improving digital skills and creating new opportunities for economic and social development.

Asia

India - Digital India

- **Overview**: A government initiative aimed at transforming India into a digitally empowered society and knowledge economy.
- **Impact**: The program has established Common Service Centers (CSCs) across rural India, providing access to digital services and training to millions of people.

Philippines - Tech4ED Centers

- **Overview**: The Technology for Education, Employment, Entrepreneurs, and Economic Development (Tech4ED) project establishes digital hubs in underserved areas.
- **Impact**: These centers provide training and access to digital resources, benefiting over 20 million Filipinos.

Latin America

Chile - Enlaces Program

- **Overview**: A government initiative to integrate ICT into education, providing schools with digital infrastructure and teacher training.
- **Impact**: The program has improved digital literacy for millions of students and teachers across the country.

Brazil - Telecentros

- **Overview**: Community telecenters that offer free access to computers and the internet, along with digital literacy training.
- **Impact**: These centers have reached millions of Brazilians, particularly in low-income areas, fostering digital inclusion.

Middle East

Jordan - ReBootKamp (RBK)

- **Overview**: A coding bootcamp that provides intensive digital skills training to young people, particularly targeting refugees and underserved communities.
- **Impact**: Graduates of the program have secured high-paying jobs in the tech industry, transforming their economic prospects.

Egypt - IT Clubs

- **Overview**: IT clubs established by the Ministry of Communications and Information Technology provide digital literacy training to people in rural areas.
- **Impact**: These clubs have trained thousands of individuals, enhancing their digital skills and employability.

Impact of Digital Literacy on Economic Development and Poverty Reduction

Digital literacy plays a critical role in economic development and poverty reduction by enabling individuals to access information, improve their skills, and participate in the digital economy. Enhanced digital literacy contributes to various socio-economic benefits.

Economic Development

1. **Job Creation and Employability**

- **Enhanced Skills**: Digital literacy equips individuals with the skills needed for modern jobs, improving employability.

Example: In India, digital literacy programs have enabled millions of people to secure jobs in the IT sector, contributing to the country's economic growth.

- **Entrepreneurship**: Digital skills enable individuals to start and grow their own businesses, creating new economic opportunities.

Example: In Nigeria, digital literacy initiatives have empowered young entrepreneurs to develop tech startups, fostering innovation and economic dynamism.

2. **Increased Productivity**

- **Efficiency**: Digital tools and skills increase productivity in various sectors, from agriculture to manufacturing.

Example: In Kenya, farmers using mobile apps for market information and weather forecasts have increased their productivity and incomes.

3. **Access to Global Markets**

- **E-commerce**: Digital literacy enables individuals and businesses to participate in e-commerce, accessing global markets and expanding their customer base.

Example: Small businesses in Brazil using e-commerce platforms have reached international customers, boosting their sales and growth.

Poverty Reduction

1. **Access to Education and Information**

- **Educational Opportunities**: Digital literacy provides access to online education and training, enabling individuals to improve their skills and knowledge.

Example: In Rwanda, online educational resources have provided students in remote areas with access to quality education, reducing educational disparities.

- **Information Access**: Digital literacy enables individuals to access information on healthcare, agriculture, and other critical areas, improving their quality of life.

Example: In Bangladesh, mobile health initiatives have provided rural communities with access to healthcare information and services.

2. **Financial Inclusion**

- **Digital Banking**: Digital literacy facilitates the use of digital banking and financial services, promoting financial inclusion and economic stability.

Example: In Kenya, the widespread use of M-Pesa has revolutionized financial transactions, providing millions with access to banking services.

3. **Empowerment of Marginalized Communities**

- **Social Inclusion**: Digital literacy empowers marginalized communities, enabling them to participate fully in the digital society.

Example: In South Africa, digital literacy programs targeting women and youth have provided them with the skills needed to access employment and educational opportunities, reducing social and economic inequalities.

Conclusion

While developing countries face significant challenges in enhancing digital literacy, there are numerous opportunities and successful initiatives that demonstrate the transformative potential of digital literacy. By addressing these challenges and leveraging these opportunities, developing countries can foster economic development, reduce poverty, and create more inclusive and equitable societies.

Chapter 17:

Ethical and Legal Considerations in Digital Literacy

Overview of Ethical Issues Related to Digital Literacy

Digital literacy encompasses not just the ability to use technology but also understanding the ethical implications of its use. Ethical issues such as privacy, surveillance, and digital rights are central to the discourse on digital literacy. These issues have far-reaching consequences, affecting individuals and societies globally.

Privacy

Data Privacy Concerns

- **Personal Information**: The collection, storage, and use of personal data by companies and governments raise significant privacy concerns. Users often share personal information online, sometimes without fully understanding how it will be used.
  - **Example**: The Facebook-Cambridge Analytica scandal highlighted how personal data could be harvested and used for political purposes without users' explicit consent.

Digital Footprint

- **Traceability**: Every online action leaves a digital footprint that can be tracked and analyzed. This raises concerns about how much information individuals inadvertently share and who has access to this information.
- **Example**: In Europe, the General Data Protection Regulation (GDPR) has been implemented to give users more control over their data and to enforce stringent data protection standards.

Surveillance

Government Surveillance

- **Mass Surveillance**: Governments in some countries use digital tools for mass surveillance, monitoring citizens' online activities under the guise of national security.

Example: In China, the government employs a sophisticated surveillance system that includes monitoring internet use and employing facial recognition technology to track individuals.

Corporate Surveillance

- **Data Tracking**: Companies often track user behavior to target advertisements and personalize services. This type of surveillance can lead to ethical dilemmas regarding consent and transparency.

Example: Google's data collection practices have been criticized for being invasive, as the company tracks users across various services to build detailed profiles for advertising purposes.

Digital Rights

Access to Information

- **Digital Divide**: Ensuring equitable access to digital tools and information is a key ethical issue. The digital divide exacerbates existing social inequalities by limiting access for certain demographics.

Example: In many parts of Africa, limited internet access restricts opportunities for education and economic advancement, underscoring the need for policies that promote digital inclusion.

Freedom of Expression

- **Censorship**: Digital platforms can be used to both promote and suppress free speech. Balancing the regulation of harmful content with the protection of free expression is a complex ethical challenge.

Example: Social media platforms like Twitter and Facebook face ongoing debates about their role in censoring content, particularly around issues of misinformation and hate speech.
-

Legal Frameworks Governing Digital Literacy, Internet Access, and Cybersecurity

Legal frameworks play a crucial role in shaping the landscape of digital literacy, ensuring that the rights of individuals are protected while fostering a safe and inclusive digital environment.

Digital Literacy

Education Policies

- **Inclusion of Digital Literacy**: Governments worldwide are increasingly incorporating digital literacy into national education policies to prepare citizens for the digital age.

Example: Finland's national curriculum includes digital literacy from an early age, ensuring that students develop critical digital skills throughout their education.

Certification and Standards

- **Standardized Training**: Establishing certification programs and standards for digital literacy can help ensure a consistent level of digital competence.

Example: The European Union's DigComp framework provides a comprehensive reference for digital competence, helping to harmonize digital literacy education across member states.

Internet Access

Universal Service Obligations

- **Ensuring Access**: Many countries have implemented policies to ensure universal access to the internet, recognizing it as a fundamental right.

Example: The Indian government's BharatNet project aims to provide high-speed internet to rural areas, bridging the digital divide.

Net Neutrality

- **Equal Access**: Net neutrality laws prevent internet service providers from discriminating against content or users, ensuring equal access to all online resources.

Example: The United States has seen significant debate over net neutrality, with varying policies under different administrations impacting how internet service providers can manage data traffic.

Cybersecurity

Data Protection Laws

- **Regulating Data Use**: Data protection laws aim to safeguard personal information and ensure that data is handled responsibly.

Example: The GDPR in Europe sets strict guidelines for data processing, giving individuals greater control over their personal data and imposing heavy fines for non-compliance.

Cybercrime Legislation

- **Combating Cybercrime**: Legal frameworks addressing cybercrime are essential for protecting users from digital threats such as hacking, fraud, and identity theft.

Example: The African Union Convention on Cyber Security and Personal Data Protection provides a comprehensive legal framework to combat cybercrime across African nations.

Role of Digital Literacy in Fostering a Responsible and Ethical Digital Society

Digital literacy is more than technical proficiency; it encompasses understanding the ethical implications of digital interactions and fostering responsible digital citizenship. Promoting digital literacy can help create a society that values privacy, security, and inclusivity.

Ethical Digital Citizenship

Critical Thinking

- **Evaluating Information**: Digital literacy education should emphasize critical thinking skills, enabling individuals to evaluate the credibility of online information and resist misinformation.

Example: Programs like News Literacy Project in the United States teach students how to discern fact from fiction, promoting responsible information consumption.

Digital Etiquette

- **Respectful Interaction**: Understanding digital etiquette is crucial for fostering respectful and constructive online interactions.

Example: The "Be Internet Awesome" program by Google educates children on how to communicate respectfully online and understand the impact of their digital actions.

Privacy Awareness

Informed Consent

- **Data Usage**: Educating individuals about how their data is collected and used helps them make informed decisions about their digital interactions.

Example: Initiatives like "MyData" in Finland promote transparency in data usage and advocate for individuals' control over their personal information.

Protective Measures

- **Security Practices**: Digital literacy should include education on basic cybersecurity practices, such as creating strong passwords and recognizing phishing attempts.

Example: Cybersecurity awareness campaigns, like those conducted during National Cybersecurity Awareness Month in the United States, aim to improve public knowledge of online safety practices.

Promoting Inclusivity

Bridging the Digital Divide

- **Equal Opportunities**: Digital literacy programs must focus on reaching underserved populations to ensure that everyone has the opportunity to benefit from digital advancements.

Example: The "Internet Saathi" program in India trains rural women to use the internet, empowering them to become community leaders in digital literacy.

Supporting Vulnerable Groups

- **Tailored Education**: Special initiatives targeting vulnerable groups, such as the elderly or people with disabilities, can help ensure that digital literacy efforts are inclusive.

Example: In Japan, programs that teach digital skills to seniors help them stay connected and access essential services, enhancing their quality of life.

Global Perspective

Digital literacy initiatives across the globe illustrate the diverse approaches to addressing ethical and legal challenges in the digital age. These initiatives highlight the importance of context-specific solutions and the need for a collaborative approach to foster an ethical digital society.

Europe

- **GDPR**: The General Data Protection Regulation sets a high standard for data protection, emphasizing individuals' rights and corporate responsibility.
- **Digital Literacy in Schools**: Countries like Estonia have integrated coding and digital skills into their national curriculum, setting a global benchmark for digital education.

North America

- **Net Neutrality**: Ongoing debates and policy changes around net neutrality in the United States illustrate the complexities of ensuring equitable internet access.
- **Digital Citizenship Programs**: Initiatives like Common Sense Media provide resources for parents and educators to teach children about responsible digital behavior.

144

Asia

- **Digital India**: This initiative aims to transform India into a digitally empowered society, focusing on infrastructure, digital literacy, and e-governance.
- **Cybersecurity Laws**: Singapore's Cybersecurity Act provides a legal framework to protect critical information infrastructure and combat cyber threats.

Africa

- **Smart Africa**: This pan-African initiative aims to leverage technology to drive economic growth and improve digital literacy across the continent.
- **Community Programs**: Local initiatives like Africa Code Week promote digital skills among youth, fostering a new generation of digital innovators.

Latin America

- **Digital Inclusion**: Programs like Brazil's Telecentros provide free access to digital tools and training in underserved communities, promoting digital inclusion.
- **Privacy Regulations**: The General Data Protection Law in Brazil (LGPD) aligns with global standards, enhancing data protection and privacy rights.

Middle East

- **Qatar's National Vision 2030**: This plan includes goals for digital transformation and education reform, emphasizing the role of digital literacy in national development.

- **Educational Initiatives**: Programs in countries like the UAE integrate digital literacy into education systems, preparing students for the digital economy.

Conclusion

Addressing the ethical and legal considerations in digital literacy requires a comprehensive approach that encompasses education, regulation, and community engagement. By fostering critical thinking, promoting privacy awareness, and ensuring inclusivity, we can build a responsible and ethical digital society that benefits all.

Closing Remarks

Throughout this book, we have embarked on a journey through the intricate landscape of digital literacy in the context of the Fourth Industrial Revolution (4IR). From exploring foundational concepts to examining advanced applications, each chapter has provided insights into how digital literacy shapes our societies, economies, and individual lives.

Digital literacy, as we have come to understand, is not merely about using technology but about understanding its ethical implications, fostering inclusivity, and preparing for the future of work and innovation. In the 4IR, characterized by rapid advancements in artificial intelligence, robotics, and the Internet of Things, digital literacy emerges as a fundamental skill set. It empowers individuals to navigate the complexities of the digital world confidently and responsibly.

Key Insights and Takeaways

Empowering Individuals and Communities

Digital literacy empowers individuals by providing access to information, education, and opportunities for personal and professional growth. It bridges gaps in traditional infrastructures and enhances social inclusion. Through initiatives and programs worldwide, we have seen marginalized communities gaining empowerment and economic opportunities through digital skills.

Driving Economic Growth

At an economic level, digital literacy drives innovation and competitiveness. Countries with robust digital literacy frameworks tend to exhibit higher productivity and economic dynamism. Digital skills are increasingly essential in the modern workforce, enabling individuals to adapt to technological changes and contribute to global markets.

Navigating Ethical and Legal Challenges

Ethical considerations, such as privacy, surveillance, and digital rights, underscore the importance of responsible digital citizenship. Legal frameworks play a crucial role in safeguarding individuals' rights and fostering a secure digital environment. Understanding these challenges is imperative as we navigate the evolving digital landscape.

Preparing for the Future

Looking ahead, the future of digital literacy holds promises and challenges. Technological advancements will continue to shape how we interact with digital tools and platforms. AI-driven educational tools and digital healthcare innovations exemplify the potential of digital literacy to transform industries and improve quality of life globally.

Global Perspectives and Collaborative Efforts

Throughout the book, we have explored global perspectives on digital literacy, recognizing that challenges and solutions vary across continents and regions. From successful national initiatives in digital education to innovative approaches in healthcare and e-commerce, collaboration and knowledge-sharing are essential for addressing digital divides and fostering digital inclusivity.

Conclusion

As we conclude this exploration of digital literacy in the 4IR, we are reminded of its transformative power and the responsibility it entails. Empowering individuals with digital skills is not merely a means to adapt to technological change but a pathway to creating a more equitable and inclusive society. By promoting digital literacy, we can harness the full potential of the Fourth Industrial Revolution for the benefit of all.

I hope this book has equipped you with the knowledge, insights, and inspiration to navigate the digital age with confidence and contribute meaningfully to shaping its future. Let us continue to embrace the opportunities and address the challenges ahead, ensuring that digital literacy remains a cornerstone of progress and human development in the 4IR and beyond.

Thank you for joining me on this journey through the world of digital literacy. Together, let us strive for a future where everyone has the skills and opportunities to thrive in the digital era.

www.ingramcontent.com/pod-product-compliance
Lightning Source LLC
LaVergne TN
LVHW051344050326
832903LV00031B/3738